# A New Theory of Justice and Other Essays

James Ward

COOL MILLENNIUM BOOKS

Published in the United Kingdom. All rights reserved. No part of this publication may be reproduced, distributed or transmitted in any form or means, without written permission.

Copyright © James Ward 2012

James Ward has asserted his right to be identified as the author of this Work in accordance with the Copyright, Designs and Patents Act 1988.

This is a work of fiction. All names, characters, and events are the product of the author's imagination, or used fictitiously. All resemblance to actual events, places, events or persons, living or dead, is entirely coincidental.

First published 2012.
This edition published 2021.

A CIP catalogue record for this book is available from the British Library.

ISBN: 978-1-913851-49-1

This book is sold subject to the condition that it shall not, by way of trade or otherwise, be lent, re-sold, hired out or otherwise circulated without the publisher's prior consent in any form of trading or cover other than that in which it is published and without a similar condition including the condition being imposed on the subsequent purchaser.

This novel was produced in the UK and uses British-English language conventions ('authorise' instead of 'authorize', 'The government are' instead of 'the government is', etc.)

To my wife

# CONTENTS

## A NEW THEORY OF JUSTICE 9

Introduction ............................................................. 9

1. The Social Contract............................................ 10

2. A New Theory of Justice.................................... 16

3. Advantages of the Theory................................. 29

4. Objections to the Theory .................................. 30

   *I. Vagueness of Applicability* ......................................... *30*

   *II. It is Merely Hobbes … Or Hegel … Or Foucault*... *36*

      *(i) Thomas Hobbes* ....................................................... *36*

      *(ii) GWF Hegel* .............................................................. *38*

      *(iii) Michel Foucault*..................................................... *40*

   *III. A Theory of Justice Which Defines Justice as a Property of Individual Decisions and Actions is Overly Reductionistic* ..................................................... *42*

   *IV. What About Rights?*................................................. *43*

5. Justice's Dark Matter: Two Puzzles ............. 45

   *(a) Kafka's Justice Machine* ........................................... *46*

- *(b) Justice by Lightning* .................................................. *50*
- 6. Conclusion .......................................................... 54

# A NEW APPROACH TO THE PHILOSOPHY OF RELIGION   55

- Introduction ........................................................... 55
- Of Teapots and Pyramids ................................... 56
- What is God? ........................................................ 60
- The God of Our Century .................................... 65
- From Does God Exist to Could God Exist ...... 70
- Is Disembodied Consciousness Possible? ..... 74
  - *1. Epiphenomenalism* ........................................................ *79*
  - *2. Intentionality* ................................................................. *85*
  - *3. Near Death Experiences* ............................................... *90*
- Final Observations ............................................... 96

# ON THE POSSIBLE VARIETIES OF CONSCIOUSNESS   98

- Kinds of Minds ..................................................... 99
- The Problem of Other Minds ......................... 101

    *1. Behaviourism* ............................................................ *102*

    *2. Mentalistic Words as Public Phenomena* ............... *104*

    *3. The Argument from Analogy* ..................................... *105*

    *4. Criteriological Accounts of Mind* ............................. *105*

    *5. The Inference to the Best Explanation* ..................... *106*

    *How Many Different Solutions Are There?* ................ *107*

## Missing Senses ................................................... 109

## Parallel Universes/ Possible Worlds/ Extra Dimensions .......................................................... 112

## A UFO Under Scrutiny ..................................... 116

## TOWARDS SOME KIND OF 'SOLUTION' TO THE PROBLEM OF EVIL     120

## FREE WILL AND LIBET'S EXPERIMENT     130

# A NEW THEORY OF JUSTICE

## Introduction

The main target in this essay is social contract theories of justice. My contention is that the 'state of nature' which they generally premise is something we cannot meaningfully talk about, since we have no uncontroversial knowledge of what is natural for human beings. Another way of putting this is to say, there is no fixed human nature.

That said, however, I believe the state of nature as found in Thomas Hobbes's work is worth discussing. Most philosophers today, whatever their reservations about Hobbes's conflation of the state of nature with 'the war of all against all', are inclined to throw both onto the scrapheap in a single gesture, finding neither particularly useful. I argue that this is a mistake. The war of all against all turns out to be a good starting point for political philosophy. Once it is accepted as one historical reality amongst others, and always a real prospect, new theoretical possibilities suggest themselves. We can dispense with talk of a state of nature whilst retaining the notion of the war of all against all as primary.

I argue that there are actually two notions of justice opposed to each other: 'harmonic' justice and 'emancipatory' justice. By 'harmonic' I do not mean to imply any value judgement, let alone a positive one. I use the word to mean: rigidly organised into an internal agreement, and adjudged by those whose interests it serves to be worth preserving unchanged in perpetuity. It is possible to have liberal regimes that fit this definition, but mostly, nowadays at least, they are despotic. 'Emancipatory' justice involves a revolt against this and is rather more self-explanatory. Strictly speaking, emancipatory justice comes as a reaction to harmonic justice. The latter is always prior.

I next try to show that injustice is the really primary term in the just-unjust dichotomy. Perhaps surprisingly, by contrast with injustice, we have only the vaguest sense of what justice is. At the moment we can only talk with precision about what we *call* it, not what it is.

This may seem inadequate to some. Surely, we urgently need to know what justice *is*. What we *call* it is a relatively trivial consideration. However, it is my contention that there are no questions about what justice *is* that cannot be answered by ethical theory. To say something is unjust in the 'real' sense is simply to say it is immoral. We therefore do not need a separate conception of justice in the substantive sense (Or rather, it will be provided incidentally, when the problems of ethics are solved). This would be the same as saying that it is not incumbent on political philosophers, as such, to provide a theory of 'real' justice *at all*; only, as we shall see, the issue is complicated by an unavoidable entanglement of the meta- and normative levels.

## 1. The Social Contract

What is justice? In the history of philosophy, the most popular answer has been, it is the successful implementation of a certain kind of social contract. And probably the most prominent theorist in this tradition – although few would go all the way with him today – is Thomas Hobbes, who in his *Leviathan* (1651), depicts humankind's natural state as a war of all against all (*bellum omnium contra omnes*), in which no one can be sure of staying alive for very long.

> "In such condition there is no place for industry, because the fruit thereof is uncertain, and consequently, no culture of the earth, no navigation, nor the use of commodities that may be imported by sea, no commodious building, no instruments of moving and removing such things as require much force, no knowledge of the face of the earth, no account of time, no arts, no letters, no society, and which is worst of all, continual fear and danger of violent death, and the life of man, solitary, poor, nasty, brutish, and short."

Such is the *summum malum*, the greatest evil. In order to avert it, human beings make a contract to create the Leviathan, a commonwealth with an absolute sovereign at its head. The sovereign has absolute power, but provides the security in which all citizens (as they now are) can pursue their own preferred ends. All of the things in the above list which the state of nature precluded, are now available. This is supposed to be (and Hobbes may well be right, if there is no alternative) sufficient compensation for the disadvantage of having a potential tyrant rule over you.

Others did not see it like that. John Locke's *Second Treatise of Government* (1689) argued that the "natural rights" of humans – something the Dutch philosopher, Hugo Grotius had discussed before Hobbes – were inalienable. (Hobbes, of course, thought people had to relinquish them to the sovereign in the process of engendering the Leviathan.)

Locke argued that government's legitimacy derives from the citizens handing over to it their right of self-defence. As a neutral judge, it undertakes to safeguard the life, liberty and property of those who have submitted to its hegemony. It derives its moral authority for that undertaking from their consent, although precisely how this consent is obtained, or renewed, are questions Locke does not address.

This was left to the Genevan philosopher, Jean-Jacques Rousseau, in his 1762 treatise, *The Social Contract*. Rousseau favoured direct democracy. Only through regular, personal participation in the real life of government can the citizens hope to ensure the creation of just laws in accordance with the 'general will', an obscure phrase which may mean something like, 'the voluntary instigation of what is in every citizen's ideal interests'.

These are all attempts to account for state justice: the question of why should I obey the state's will as expressed through its laws. The answer given is, because I am involved in a hypothetical contract to do so, from which I reap real benefits.

However, the most celebrated modern version of a contract theory - John Rawls's 1971 'veil of ignorance', in

*A Theory of Justice* – isn't about why I should obey the state's laws. It is an attempt to solve the problem of distributive justice: the allocation of goods and services in society. Rawls starts off from an 'original position' in which the participants are behind the said veil of ignorance.

> "No one knows his place in society, his class position or social status, nor does anyone know his fortune in the distribution of natural assets and abilities, his intelligence, strength, and the like. I shall even assume that the parties do not know their conceptions of the good or their special psychological propensities. The principles of justice are chosen behind a veil of ignorance."

Rawls thinks that the participants would act to minimise the chances of their ending up in a disadvantageous position. They would arrange social and economic inequalities to benefit the most disadvantaged members of society and ensure that public offices and employment opportunities are open to all.

Contract theories, of justice, as might be expected, suffer from alleged common defects. In a state of nature such as Hobbes depicts, it is doubtful whether the actors would have developed the language or social skills necessary to make a wide-ranging contract of the Leviathan type. His are abstract individuals capable of speculative reasoning, distinguishing long-term and short-term goals and recognising psychological similarities in other beings of like biological constitution. They seem to be socialised before socialisation.

Locke and Rousseau, in fact, do not pretend otherwise. In Locke's version of the theory, the state of nature is not a state of war, although war often occurs in it. It is defined as "a state of perfect freedom of acting and disposing of [people's] own possessions and persons as they think fit within the bounds of the law of nature". In it, an individual is, "absolute lord of his own person and possessions, equal to the greatest, and subject to no body".

Rousseau goes even further. Man, in his natural state, is good and only corrupted by society. In *Emile* (1762), he writes, "Our natural passions are few in number; they are the means to freedom, they tend to self-preservation. All those which enslave and destroy us have another source; nature does not bestow them on us; we seize on them in her despite."

Of course, feminist, multiculturalist and postmodern thinkers have focused on these shortcomings. The abstract participant in the social contract is none other than the author in question himself: a white, male oppressor. ('Oppressor' here is not always hyperbole. Locke owned shares in the Royal Africa Company and the Bahama Adventurers, both slave-trading enterprises, and eventually sold his shares at a profit.) Feminists such as Carole Pateman, in *The Sexual Contract* (1988), may well be right in claiming that the social contract, as Locke, Hobbes and Rousseau envisaged it, presupposes another invisible, patriarchal contract holding sway within the family, as well as in prostitution and in surrogate motherhood.

One common theme of all such criticisms is that social contract theories do not devote enough space to the problem of *in*justice. In order to understand injustice, they often say, you need a historical understanding of concrete social groups. It is no use saying that society $x$ is founded on a hypothetical social contract, if social subgroup $y$ has always experienced discrimination within that society. Obviously, there is some way in which $y$ has been, and is, excluded from the contract.

The contract theorist has an answer to this, of course. Yes, in any actually existing society, you will probably find that certain groups are excluded on some level, but that is what injustice is. Contract theory identifies it as such and says what its remedy consists in. Injustice is exclusion and its remedy consists in the implementation or restoration of full participation. Obviously, abstract philosophical theories cannot usually be expected to supply solutions for every particular real-life problem, especially where there are a potentially infinite number of these.

We could pursue this discussion, but there may be little point, since any version of it we develop here will be but a re-write of earlier versions, all better developed. The point of this chapter lies in a different place: it is to develop a theory of justice which I believe avoids the sting of those criticisms of the social contract I have outlined, and which opens up new vistas for the concept of justice itself.

I will explain what I mean by the last clause presently. For the time being, I shall follow Hobbes's style of presentation in *Leviathan*: that is, I shall begin by setting out the theory, then responding to what I anticipate will be the main lines of attack upon it.

## 2. A New Theory of Justice

Let us revisit one of the questions from the introduction: what constitutes a state of nature for humans?

The simple answer is, we don't know. Human beings are social animals, so, given sufficient subsistence and a congenial enough climate, their state of nature may well involve a sophisticated culture and technology. Equally, there may be no such thing; or everything may be a state of nature. Is the Millennium Dome natural? Is the London Eye? Philosophers are used to asking such questions, especially when they are put in the awkward position of having to entertain prospective students. But how can we possibly begin to answer them?

Much more interesting is Hobbes's *bellum omnium contra omnes*. Human societies *do* break down completely from time to time, and a complete absence of justice *may* become the norm. What is interesting to ask is how we get from there to a society that manifests any kind of justice. We know the answer Hobbes gave. Humans come together and make a contract.

I contend that what happens instead is a radical restructuring in accordance with strength. Human beings are biological creatures. Even if all start from a position of rough equality, survival of the fittest suggests that certain people will be faster to grab weapons, more proficient at using them, less punctilious about having recourse to them. Others will recognise this, and some of those others will put themselves at the service of these men. They nearly always *will* be men, because the human body is the original weapon and on the whole men are heavier and taller than women, and immune to pregnancy.

What will happen, in other words, is that the war of all against all will play itself out, by means of a perhaps protracted period of violent bloodletting, to a condition of absolute tyranny, or more likely, tyrannies: terroristic rule by warlords whose chief allies are perhaps their own family members.

Worst off in this transition will be women, because they are integral to the family (so crucial to control), and mostly more physically vulnerable than men (so easier to control), a source of sexual gratification and labour-power to men, and easy for men to identify. Every effort will be made to ensure that their submission is complete by incarcerating them in the home, or brutally punishing some as a lesson to the others. Ultimately, the means of domination will be physical, but once the women have been enculturated to accept and, where possible, embrace their condition, this may only rarely be necessary.

Next worst off will be minorities, especially those marked out by some bodily feature such as skin colour or physiognomy. Where it is desired to create slaves, minorities may even serve that purpose, unless there are sufficient prisoners of war or foreign captives, although even these may be given corporeal features: tattoos, for example, or brands.

Insofar as the rival warlords manage to come to a mutual understanding, this will not usually be by means of a contract, but by a *de facto* recognition of the extreme cost of war at the expense of consolidation. Territories will be marked out, trespassers will be eliminated and everyone will accept that.

But not always. Sometimes, wars will result in the absolute destruction of A by B along with the annexation of A's territory and its resources.

Notice, though, that we have now passed from a condition of absolute chaos to a situation of relative order. In principle (though perhaps never in practice), once the bloodbath is over, providing everyone beneath the sovereign is absolutely obedient, they will live, and might even prosper to an extent, since it is not usually in the sovereign's interest to keep his subjects in absolute penury.

Here, now, we approach the two rival conceptions of justice. The sovereign's notion of justice will be *justice as harmony*. That 'harmony' (an aesthetic rather than a moral term) will be exhibited in the hierarchical social order he establishes: the sovereign, the militiamen, the citizens (usually subdivided by sex), the slaves. Given enough time, this will almost certainly become a religious conception. In any case, it only really becomes *internally nameable* as 'justice' once the relationship between the different tiers in society is expressed in abstract terms, and efforts are expended to maintain it in stasis. Not "Charles has absolute authority over Oliver" but "The English king, of which Charles I is an example, is divinely authorised to command his subjects, of which Oliver Cromwell is an example". We have something like a universalised prescription to the effect that no one is ever to disrupt the harmony in question. Relationships of harmonic justice can usually be exhaustively described using the language of responsibilities.

In her 1938 *Meditation on Obedience and Liberty*, the French thinker and mystic, Simone Weil, wrote:

> "That a number of men should submit themselves to a single man through fear of being killed by him is astonishing enough; but what are we to make of it when they remain submissive to him to the point of dying at his orders? When there are at least as many risks attached to obedience as to rebellion, how is obedience maintained? ... Is there at the present time, over the whole of the earth's surface, a single mind that can conceive even vaguely how it is that one man in the Kremlin has the power to cause any head whatever to fall within the confines of the Russian frontiers?"

Social contract theories have difficulty explaining this phenomenon, of course, although it does not quite refute them. The answer perhaps lies in the strength of the ruler and the fact that the harmonic relationship is defined in abstract terms, creating either (a) the impression that everyone can in theory achieve a position of lesser vulnerability or greater enjoyment – even if, as in rigid theocracies, that happens after death, or (b) the impression that the harmony in question is somehow natural, and thus right-in-itself. Of course, Marxism was well suited to creating both sorts of impression, which is probably why it was the favoured ideology of harmonic elites all over the globe for so long.

Most ancient notions of justice are harmonic. Someone upsets the order of the universe, even unknowingly, and 'justice' is done to the extent that it is restored. This is the justice of Oedipus; it is the fate of Sodom and Gomorrah; it is the reason Uzzah is struck dead by God for trying to steady the Ark of the Covenant in 2 Samuel; it is the justice of *The Republic*, in which a good society is ordered like a good soul; it is the Great Chain of Being; it is the Divine Right of kings (into which justice as Divine Command, and probably Natural Law too, can be completely dissolved).

But harmonic justice does not have to be tyrannical, or the response to a war of all humans against all other humans. It is equally likely to have its roots in the war of all humans against *nature:* that is, in a world in which resources are hard to come by, predators are fearsome, and humans have to work unceasingly to survive. Probably all prehistoric human societies were harmonic: social positions within the hierarchy, and the exact nature of the hierarchy itself, must have been more or less immutable, and were probably sanctioned by supposed ancestral, or even supernatural, authority.

It is perhaps tempting to say harmonic justice is simply another word for conservatism, but the truth is that harmonic systems may be very short lived, and the social relations they institute may be widely perceived as revolutionary. More seriously, the term 'conservatism' does not really explain anything. Amongst other things, all conservative cultures favour traditional family roles and at least a *prima facie* suspicion of outsiders, but in other respects they may be wildly divergent and even mutually hostile. Calling both conservative is a categorisation after the event, based on such characteristics. By contrast, the first form of harmonic justice is the overcoming of the *bellum omnium contra omnes* by means of the survival of the fittest, and the average physically fittest are men and majority ethnic groups. The lure of conservatism, on this analysis, is the lure of the definitive, permanent-for-all-practical-purposes, resolution of the war of all against all, because some people, whenever and wherever they are, are apt to see the slippery slope to that war everywhere.

The second form of justice we must consider is *justice as emancipation,* and it has much less of a written history. It is the justice of Spartacus, of Jael in the book of Judges; it is the hidden history of wives who kill violent husbands, slaves who turn on their masters, citizens who assassinate despots. Sometimes, the liberty sought may be personal; otherwise, it may be on behalf of one's social or ethnic group. Once again, it only becomes justice to the extent that it can be expressed in abstract terms. Not "Jane should kill John" but "Women, of which group Jane is an example, have the right to kill their physically abusive husbands, of which group John is an example, in the heat of the assault." Relationships of emancipatory justice can often, but not always, be wholly translated into the language of morality (which is not to say that, in such circumstances, they *are* moral). Whereas harmonic justice is static, emancipatory justice is dynamic. There is sometimes an intimate link between the two: acts of emancipatory justice may occasionally be inspired by the desire for a different type of harmony to the one that prevails.

In any case, both types of justice fail as moral systems the closer each approaches to purity. A society that only exhibited harmonic justice might be admirable - a perfect mechanism of efficiency and self-correction, like an auto-regulating clock – but not primarily moral. All individual acts of justice within it would exactly fit the definition Cephalus gives in Book I of *The Republic*: speaking the truth (assuming here that there are no moral facts, and thus no 'moral truth') and paying one's debts. The 'just' behaviour of citizens of such a system might be no more moral than the allegedly "eusocial" behaviour of ants.

By the same token, pure emancipatory justice would also fail to be moral. It might look, at first, as if emancipatory justice is a kind of potential harmonic justice, insofar as it is tending towards something like the (harmonious) Kingdom of Ends. But this is a mistake. It does not necessarily draw the line at killing, and it is not necessarily idealistic: it has its essential being in the moment. No, what the emancipatory agent is after is first and foremost – though other considerations may accompany it - what Isaiah Berlin (1909-97) called *negative freedom*: the freedom from certain constraints or obstacles.

But complete freedom from constraints is a kind of anarchy. Max Stirner's thinking in *The Ego and Its Own* (1845) is perhaps the ultimate expression of emancipatory justice, as Albert Camus seemed to acknowledge in *The Rebel* (1951). "Revolution is aimed at new arrangements; insurrection leads us no longer to let ourselves be arranged, but to arrange ourselves, and set no glittering hopes on 'institutions.'" We are back to the *bellum omnium contra omnes*. Something like this is recognised by Plato in Book VIII of *The Republic*. Tyranny arises naturally out of democracy, but only after the war of all against all has paid a visit. "By degrees the anarchy finds a way into private houses, and ends by getting among the animals and infecting them ... and all things are just ready to burst with liberty".

Given that societies strongly marked by harmonic justice will, in practice, always give rise to attempts at emancipatory justice, and that both, rigorously and exclusively pursued, will, to the extent that they triumph, always lead to non-moral states of affairs, it looks as if what we generally call justice – that is to say what *philosophers* call justice when they are writing treatises on the subject: essentially a moral category – must somehow emerge in the ongoing struggle between the two opposed extremes. Sometimes - perhaps more often than not - their relationship will be one of war: buildings will be razed, people will be killed (and yet the war is waged by the 'just' against the 'unjust'). At its most sophisticated, it will occur in dialogue (as Jürgen Habermas has it in, eg, *The Inclusion of the Other: Studies in Political Theory* (1998)), in a democracy. But it is never entirely friendly. And no state is ever entirely legitimated by it, because there is no social contract, not even a hypothetical one, only an open-ended dialectic.

It might seem, at first sight, as if we can end the indeterminacy here by appealing to something like Adam Smith's and David Hume's Ideal Observer. Someone who is impartial, benevolent and appraised of all the relevant facts. Maybe he or she would be able to look at a given situation, appraise the balance of harmonic against emancipatory justice, assess the moral features, and pronounce definitively on the 'real' justice or otherwise of the propositions under consideration.

However, in practice, Ideal Observers seem either hopelessly inadequate (because too real - as Alexander Broadie puts it in, *The Cambridge Companion to Adam Smith* (2006), "[Smith's] impartial spectator is not the ideal, but only the best, for all its many faults, that we can imagine") or genuinely inconceivable (because too *un*real - as in Roderick Firth, where "X is right" means "If there was a person who was omniscient, omnipercipient, disinterested as dispassionate, but in other respects normal, then he would have a certain experience (feel approval, experience an apparent requiredness, etc.) with respect to X" (1952)).

Anyway, and this is a crucial point: 'justice' is essentially a response to 'injustice'; 'injustice', or the perception of it, always comes first. When we live under a just regime, or we encounter a just society, we hardly ever describe it as such: we call it 'tolerant' or 'transparent' or 'democratic' or 'sustainable' or 'open' or 'liberal', or all of the above. But when injustice appears, we always name it. Normally, the positive term in any binary duality is thought to be the one which explains the negative, but injustice-justice is one of those rare cases in which the reverse is true. In practice, justice is usually the righting of an injustice.

And it is never so much *defined* as simply recognised. And it interests us. When Odysseus slaughters Penelope's suitors on his return to Ithaca, we are being invited by Homer to recognise the remedying of an injustice; or to give a banal example, when the prince's slipper fits Cinderella's foot. There is nearly always drama created by the recognition, however much we may disagree, personally, with the veracity of the 'recognition'.

By contrast, as we have just said, when what is commonly taken to be justice reigns supreme, it is so humdrum it is hardly worth talking about. Why? Because the goods it makes possible then come into view – travel, creativity, prosperity – and these are infinitely more enthralling than their mere precondition. 'Justice' is chiefly of interest when it is being restored. And it probably always contains an element of "getting your own back."

Which requires the presence of injustice. Of course, there are usually an unlimited number of ways any one thing can be not-$x$. From one point of view, it is the absence of harmony (even if, during such an absence, everyone's desires are ultimately fulfilled - which seems unlikely - no one knows what quite to expect next, so the 'injustice' of undue anxiety is inflicted). From this point of view, it is 'just' for Sita, in The Ramayana, to step into a fire to prove her fidelity to Rama, even though from a modern perspective it looks outrageous: in the 'just' interpretation, her action restores the harmony proper to the social-and-divine order through a public vindication of the harmonious relations thought to constitute their foundation. From the emancipatory point of view, injustice is the absence of freedom.

Whatever one's perspective, it seems as if justice in practice is primarily about *decisions*. The reason has to do with the self-eliminating nature – which we have already described - of both harmonic and emancipatory justice. Under conditions of *pure* harmonic justice there are no hard decisions to be made: since everyone immediately recognises their debts and pays them (even out of fear), they are made more or less automatically; under pure emancipatory justice, the only meaningful decisions are made with a view to negating the situation, since there is no stable background: we are in the world of Kant's lying promiser. In the struggle between the two types of justice, however, real decisions have to be made and it is these, or the result of them, to which the labels "just" or "unjust" primarily get attached. Later on, we shall have cause to modify this conclusion slightly (see "Justice by Lightning", below). By way of anticipation, I should underline the word "seems" and "primarily" in the sentence that begins this paragraph.

It is worth noticing that there is probably what might be called a *false deontology* in both the harmonic and emancipatory conceptions of justice: proponents of both may think, and insist, that their actions are universalisable, when they are not.

Any allegedly unjust *state of affairs* is capable of being analysed into the constituent decisions which gave rise to it and sustain it. This is why, for example, the state of affairs in the US Deep South in the 1960s can be described as unjust, while the state of affairs in Indonesia as a result of the Asian tsunami of 2004 cannot (except insofar as human negligence and cruelty exacerbated the situation). Both may contain equal amounts of human suffering, but one was the result of decisions, the other was not. On this reading, laws are simply meta-decisions; decisions, embodied in statute, to henceforth identify all incidences of category-*x* acts in such-and-such a way, and as falling under such-and-such a rubric.

On such an analysis, no persons can ever be truly invisible, because all the means necessary to illumine their condition are to hand: we simply trace the genealogy of the decisions. Everyone in society is where he or she is for a reason, because of rulings which have been, and are being, made. And although we call them "decisions", they might, depending on the circumstances, more appropriately be described as diktats or decrees. They constitute the front-lines of the struggle between the two types of justice, and their implementation usually represents at least a partial victory for one or other, since each decision has to be understood in terms of its antecedents. In order to find out why any particular person or persons is the subject of injustice, it will usually be necessary, as we remarked a moment ago, to do history.

Of course, although justice is primarily about decisions, that cannot be the end of the story. Decisions issue in actions. So justice is also a property of certain actions, although it is always the decisions that are fundamental, since an instance of behaviour which was not willed is either fortunate or unfortunate, not just or unjust. To put it in philosophical terms, it is an event rather than an action.

One important consequence of all this is to dismantle the distinction between distributive, commutative and retributive justice. In reality, there are only decisions, to which the labels 'just' or 'unjust' more or less apply. But they apply after the fact.

Of the three, distribution and commutation are probably best suited to illustrate this, because they are value-free terms. As regards the former, I might distribute some leaflets in a meeting, and for the latter, I might give someone a frivolous present in a White Elephant Gift Exchange. Retribution is more difficult because it is already a moral term, but one is tempted to say that 'retribution' and 'retributive justice' are synonyms. Moreover, imagine a world in which all retribution took the form of denying the victims access to certain goods. Probably no good purpose could be served by asking whether the privation was a matter of retributive or distributive justice. The only useful question would be whether the decision that resulted in the actions that brought about the situation was just or not.

And of course, arguably, most just or unjust decisions are like this: they straddle at least two of the three traditional categories. The point is not that we *can't* classify just decisions and actions into these groups – obviously, we can. Such a thing is clearly useful for the purposes of training criminal and corporate lawyers, judges, civil servants and government legislators. But for philosophers, the distinction muddies the issue.

Before I finish this outline and go on to look at some of the potential advantages of the theory I have propounded, I should include a caveat. I think there are probably hardly any people whose view of justice is purely emancipatory or purely harmonic, and very few historical movements that have been exclusively one or the other. Most emancipators will have a notion of the positive freedom they are aiming for, and thus their own vision of the harmonic society, which may be entirely egalitarian. Most harmonic thinkers, apart from the sovereign, will find themselves constrained to behave against their wishes from time to time, and will long for emancipation.

## 3. Advantages of the Theory

There are several advantages of the theory I have proposed over traditional social contract theories. These are:

1. It does not require an assumption about human nature, ie, in the case of the social contract, that all people are self-interested or (in Rousseau's case) that they are good. It is enough for the present theory that *some* people are self-interested. It recognises the fact of variation within the human species.

2. It does not posit an ideal state of affairs in the past, even a hypothetical one, and construe our endeavours as more or less successful attempts to recover it.

3. It does not preclude the possibility that humans may "advance" beyond the position of stalemate to something more preferable, eg, the face-to-face socialised community of the anarchists or traditional communists. While one outcome of the struggle between emancipatory and harmonic justice may be a congenial truce of sorts, such a thing will always be fluid, never fixed.

4. It applies to domestic and global relations equally. In fact, global affairs are better understood as a struggle

between harmonic justice (the attempted imposition of order by one state on the whole, with itself at the apex, either through empire-building, annexation or engineering relations of economic hegemony), and emancipatory justice (attempts to resist and undermine this, sometimes perhaps in the quest for a different model of harmony). Of course, since the struggle between harmonic and emancipatory justice is always occurring both domestically and internationally simultaneously, this gives us the tools for construction of something like a theory of class struggle, although such a theory will not always be applicable.

5. It is more consistent with what we know of natural selection and survival of the fittest. Especially where resources are scarce, creatures will fight to stay alive. Some sort of stable ecosystem will evolve as a standoff between competitors.

6. It chimes with empirical history. It informs and is informed by it.

## 4. Objections to the Theory

There are lots of objections that can be raised against all the above. I shall consider them in order of importance, beginning with the most serious.

### I. *Vagueness of Applicability*

The first objection states that the theory does not do what a theory of justice should. It neither enables the reader to recognise a just decision, nor a just condition of society, nor to remedy real-world states of affairs to the extent that they disappoint. To put it another way: the theory tells us is that there are two *notions* of justice at odds with each other, but it does not say how *actual* justice emerges. All the theory offers is an engaging creation myth for 'justice' with no practical applicability.

Supporters of this objection will hold that what a theory of justice should do is exemplified by Rawls, Hobbes, Locke, Rousseau or John Stuart Mill's famous "harm principle".

I think this objection is partly correct, but that there are several problems with the approach my hypothetical objector takes.

To begin with, I do not think there is any doubt that there really is a difference between, on the one hand, what justice *really is* and, on the other, what people *call and have called* justice. The essence of the vagueness objection is that I am writing a theory of the latter, whereas the important history of the discipline, and its meaningful future, consists in theories of the former. I accept the first part of this accusation: I really am writing a theory of the latter. But in my defence, I doubt it is possible to give a theory of what justice really is. When we imagine we are doing so, what we are actually writing about is what *we call* justice. Put it this way. No theory of justice can really ignore the fact that lots of things we now regard as abhorrent were once considered just. Those things have to be identified and accounted for, and they inevitably raise the question, if we were *once* wrong about what justice is, how do we know we are not *still* wrong? The question of what justice *is* then gets swallowed up by an enquiry into the appositeness of the term. This can, and often does, result in a kind of conceptual mishmash in which nothing is quite what it seems.

The strength of the theory I am proposing is that it allows us to separate the two issues: it distinguishes between what we call justice and what justice is. The latter, it effectively relinquishes its property rights to, despatching it instead to that branch of philosophy called normative ethics. In other words, we do not need a theory of justice to do what the objector requires of it: just a theory of morality. Indeed, I would go further than this. There is nothing a theory of justice could do, to discover what 'real' justice is, that has not already been attempted by ethical philosophers such as Aristotle, Kant or Mill. Even social contract theory is really an ethical theory before it is a political one. We only think otherwise because it had its historical origins in political theory. In other words, it continues to be primarily associated with political theory for traditional, not philosophical, reasons.

But even social contract theory is mainly an account of what we call justice, not what justice is.

Most social contract theories take their cue from the supposed fact of human beings' self-interest. They are all essentially variants of Glaucon's brilliant summary in Book II of *The Republic*:

> "They say that to do injustice is, by nature, good; to suffer injustice, evil; but that the evil is greater than the good. So when men have both done and suffered injustice and have had experience of both, not being

able to avoid the one and obtain the other, they think they had better agree among themselves to have neither. Hence there arise laws and mutual covenants, and that which is ordained by law is termed by them lawful and just. This they affirm to be the origin and nature of justice. It is a mean, or compromise, between the best of all which is to do injustice and not be punished, and the worst of all which is to suffer injustice without the power of retaliation. Justice, being at a middle point between the two, is tolerated not as a good, but as the lesser evil, and honoured by reason of the inability of men to do injustice. For no man who is worthy to be called a man would ever submit to such an agreement if he were able to resist. He would be mad if he did."

This sort of theory – the sort that discovers the roots of justice in self-interest - is arguably really a theory of ideal prudence: the prudent thing to do is form a contract. To return to Rawls, if I choose to adopt the liberty and equality principles from behind the veil of ignorance, ie, because I have no idea where in society I might end up, then I am choosing them out of fear. So we are back to Glaucon. This is not so much 'justice as fairness' as 'justice as tremulous pragmatism'. But tremulous pragmatism is simply what we *call* justice here.

'Real' justice can only be described in moral terms. Rawls attempts this to an extent. Arguably, however, political philosophers are not best suited to solve questions of ethics. To the extent that we are looking for 'real' justice, it is an ethical/ moral problem. Its solution – if there can ever be one – lies within a different field. It is the greatest happiness of the greatest number; or it is the expression of a universalised maxim; or it comes under some other account of morality, possibly a contractual one.

However, we should not go too far with this. Attempts to understand justice in *exclusively* moral terms run into two problems:

(1) Firstly, unless the resulting account is to sink in the swamp of relativism – where there is no 'Justice' as such, only different 'justices' (and we are back to what we *call* justice) - it requires an absolutist theory of morality. But justice is primarily about consequences, so we seem to require a theory of morality that is *also* consequentialist. This is a very tall order. (Rawls attempts to draw on Kant, but Kantian ethics probably doesn't cover all the necessary bases. Rule Utilitarianism might be another option.)

(2) How to explain those uses of 'justice' which seem more concerned with the re-establishment of an eternally valid social order, than with the attempt to do anything 'moral'. This is the usage within which Prometheus, Phaeton, Cassiopeia and King Saul are all punished justly. They have overstepped the bounds, and we can only very artificially make sense of their treatment, and even the behaviour which provoked it, in the language and conventions of morality. The truth is, we don't need a moral interpretation here at all: only a mechanical one. The machine (which is the natural order) has malfunctioned because one of its parts – Prometheus/ Phaeton/ Cassiopeia – is defective: justice is nothing more than the repair of the whole by means of the removal of the faulty part. If 'justice' is a term with a

long-standing *de facto* application to this sort of scenario, then the moral interpretation must overlook much of its historical meaning. Of course, it is always open to us to make a word mean what we want it to mean, but usually only by ignoring its divergent uses, and where those latter are extensive we run the risk of taking language on holiday.

Arguably, talk of harmonic and emancipatory justice avoids both these problems. We can describe justice exhaustively in this 'meta-' sense, and leave the moral notion of justice for normative applications. In that case, the exact meaning of the term, in those contexts, becomes the concern philosophers of ethics. We can accept (provisionally) that it *has* a moral meaning, without feeling the need to specify precisely what it is; it is outside the sphere of our expertise. As mentioned above, the moral meaning of the term justice would probably have to be found in a consequentialist theory, rather than one concerned with motives. However, the latter is not impossible: divine justice might be simply an emanation of the will of the deity. Ultimately, as I have suggested, it may need an absolutist-consequentialist theory. I leave it to the reader to decide whether this is an oxymoron.

A further caveat. The distinction between the meta- and the normative level here does not resemble the same distinction in the field of ethics. In meta-ethics there is a rigid borderline between, on the one hand, questions about the meaning of words like 'good' and 'ought', and, on the other, the practical question of how to achieve a morally good outcome. In the field of justice, the 'meta-' level is never wholly independent of the business of achieving justice in reality. Considerations of harmony and emancipation keep encroaching on real-life discussions of justice and injustice in a way that considerations of necessary emotion, or (to give another example) intuition do not usually encroach on ethics. This inevitably raises the question whether the struggle between harmony and emancipation can really be described as a 'meta-' level at all. In some ways, it clearly can't. We shall return to this later.

## II. It is Merely Hobbes ... Or Hegel ... Or Foucault

This class of objections goes like this. "What you have described in merely a re-hash of Hobbes's 'Sovereignty of Acquisition', as discussed in Book II, chapters 17-21 of *Leviathan*. Or it is a re-hash of Hegel's account of 'Lordship and Bondage' in Part IV of *The Phenomenology of Mind*. Or it is derivative of Michel Foucault's views on justice."

It is certainly true that the theory I am proposing here has lots in common with what Hegel and Foucault have to say, but I think less so with Hobbes. In any case, we can look at each in turn.

### (i) Thomas Hobbes

According to Hobbes, a ruler can achieve sovereignty in two ways. Firstly, through contract (or institution), when people agree to hand themselves over to a sovereign power to protect their most vital interests. This is Sovereignty by Institution, and its consequence is the transition from a state of nature to a commonwealth.

The second type of sovereignty occurs when the sovereign uses force to compel a group to submit to him. This is Sovereignty of Acquisition. As Hobbes puts it in chapter 20 of *Leviathan*:

> "A commonwealth by acquisition is that where the sovereign power is acquired by force; and it is acquired by force when men singly, or many together by plurality of voices, for fear of death, or bonds, do authorise all the actions of that man, or assembly, that hath their lives and liberty in his power."

Hobbes distinguishes two forms of Sovereignty by Acquisition: by generation (having largely to do with parents and children) and by conquest. It is the latter which concerns us here.

> "Dominion acquired by conquest, or victory in war, is that which some writers call despotical from Despotes, which signifieth a lord or master, and is the dominion of the master over his servant. And this dominion is then acquired to the victor when the vanquished, to avoid the present stroke of death, covenanteth, either in express words or by other sufficient signs of the will, that so long as his life and the liberty of his body is allowed him, the victor shall have the use thereof at his pleasure."

I will not claim that my proposal does not exhibit an overlap with this idea, but obviously there are lots of differences, and most of them will already be obvious. Crucially, in the theory I have set out, there is no covenant. The harmony of the system is never a necessary arrangement of necessary parts: its precise nature may fluctuate, providing the control exercised from the top - or by tradition, or custom, or by external forces such as scarcity and the danger of predators - remains constant. I may survive if I make myself sufficiently invisible, but even then, in some circumstances, a wholly unforeseeable accident might pique the sovereign's paranoia, and I may be hunted down and sent hurtling into the abyss. In which case, I am the victim of state terrorism directed at its own people.

In addition, on the Hobbesian thesis, there is no sense of a struggle between harmonic and emancipatory justice, nor of specific 'just' decisions as emerging from this conflict.

*(ii) GWF Hegel*

Hegel's account of the Lord and Bondman is set out in in Part IV of *The Phenomenology of Mind*. In it, two pre-reflective selves meet and, to the extent that one recognises the other as similar to himself, ie, subjectively real, he attempts to impose his will on that other. The other will return the attempted negation, and a struggle ensues. The upshot is that "this trial by death ... cancels both the truth which was to result from it, and therewith the certainty of self altogether." What next follows is thus the second best option, the enslavement of one by the other, with the paradoxical consequence that the triumphant Lord becomes dependent on his Bondsman for recognition. Moreover, the Bondsman creates products for the Lord, and the former realises his self-consciousness through them. Meanwhile, the Lord becomes dependent on the Bondsman for produce. All this enables the Bondsman to revive the struggle.

Naturally, the precise significance of this story has been disputed. In addition to the crucial question of what the two selves are meant to represent (children, or 'savages' or nations, or societies), there is the linked question of what more general point Hegel was making. In Alexander Kojeve's influential lectures on Hegel, delivered in Paris between 1933 and 1939, the story shows that full self-consciousness can only arise where there are neither masters nor slaves. Simone de Beauvoir used it to represent the struggle between the sexes in *The Second Sex* (1949), and Fritz Fanon applied it to race relations in *Black Skin, White Masks* (1952). One thing everyone agrees, however, is that Hegel's story is mainly about subjectivity-in-context.

In the account of justice I have given, by contrast, the *bellum omnium contra omnes* comes (logically) first, then harmonic justice, then emancipatory justice. In Hegel, both master and slave arrive on the scene together; one takes control, then the other. The war of all against all, insofar as it occurs in Hegel's thinking here at all (which it does - "each must aim at the death of the other"), occurs whenever the protagonists are evenly matched, not as a precondition.

But this may seem premature. Since we claimed, above, that "pure" harmonic justice and "pure" emancipatory justice are both – paradoxically - non-just in the conventional moral sense, then to the extent that each persists in pressing its agenda, we must be entitled to conclude that here, as well, "each must aim at the death of the other".

The problem with this analysis, however, is that, in its haste to assimilate harmonic and emancipatory justice to the story of the Lord and Bondsman, it has to conceive the two as fully discreet movements. I refer the reader to the caveat I offered in the final paragraph of chapter 2. Most people's and most groups' outlooks are a mixture of the harmonic and the emancipatory. And of course, the present theory allows for the existence of such a thing as 'real' justice: it just consigns it to the province of conventional ethical theory.

*(iii) Michel Foucault*

In an International Philosophers' Project debate with Noam Chomsky in 1971, Foucault said:

> "It seems to me that the idea of justice in itself is an idea which in effect has been invented and put to work in different types of societies as an instrument of a certain political and economic power or as a weapon against that power. But it seems to me that, in any case, the notion of justice itself functions within a society of classes as a claim made by the oppressed class and as justification for it."

I do not propose to spend too much time discussing Foucault, firstly because there is significant resemblance between his theory of Power and Hegel's story of the Master and Bondsman (and also with Nietzsche's notion master and slave morality in *Beyond Good and Evil*), and secondly because Foucault himself does not explicitly discuss justice very much. It is nevertheless easy to construct a Foucaultian theory of justice from Foucault's own assertions, in the same debate, that "rather than thinking of the social struggle in terms of 'justice', one has to emphasise justice in terms of the social struggle" and "one doesn't speak in terms of justice, but in terms of power". Claims for justice, he apparently thinks, are disguised claims for power and themselves part of the struggle for power.

The problem, with this, I think, is that it is simplistic. Claims for justice have to be believed to be universalisable, or they are mere noises. On Foucault's analysis, probably because it is so underdeveloped, there is no distinction between a claim for justice and a claim for power. I am therefore not convinced that his account represents a great advance on Thrasymachus' in *The Republic*, the only difference being that whereas Thrasymachus says, "justice is nothing else than the interest of the stronger", Foucault would probably say "Justice is nothing else than the interest of power", taking into account that both Lord and Bondsman have power.

Which is fine, but it doesn't get us very far. If claims for justice are just expressions of approval or disapproval of another's power-claims, we have come no further than emotivism.

What I am suggesting however, is that there are limits to what can be claimed in the name of justice by the different parties in a dispute. Those limits are imposed by what can be defeasibly universalised. Claims to justice are not *ad hoc* tokens in a struggle for domination. They have a kind of claimed truth-value, so that they may well, on occasion, rebound damagingly on the claimant. I am not convinced that we get that in Foucault (or more obviously, in Nietzsche).

## *III. A Theory of Justice Which Defines Justice as a Property of Individual Decisions and Actions is Overly Reductionistic*

In his extremely readable *A Very Short Introduction to Political Philosophy* (Oxford 2003), Professor David Miller includes a paragraph which may help illumine this particular objection.

> "Critics such as the Austrian economist-cum-philosopher Friedrich Hayek argued that there was a fundamental error involved even in talking about social justice in the first place. According to Hayek, justice is fundamentally a property of individual actions: an action is unjust when it violates a general rule that a society has put in place to allow its members to cooperate with each other – so, for instance, theft is unjust because it violates a rule protecting property. But if we look at how resources – money, property, employment opportunities, and so forth – are distributed across a society, we cannot describe this distribution as either just or unjust, since it results not from the actions or decisions of a single agent, but from the actions and decisions of millions of separate people, none of whom intended to create

this or any other distributive outcome in particular." (p85)

Miller disagrees with Hayek. He points out that distribution depends on institutions we have brought into being. Since we can choose to alter those institutions by democratic action, we can make the distribution of goods more or less just. Obviously, we can only do that if we can talk about just and unjust distributions beforehand.

But even if this were not the case, simply because justice is primarily about decisions and actions, it does not mean the term cannot apply on a higher descriptive level. A dog's fur coat may be made entirely of individual brown hairs, but that does not mean we cannot talk about 'the brown dog'.

While justice is primarily about decisions and actions, the reference of those decisions may also be holistic phenomena, such as when I make a decision to buttress the harmony of my society by authorising repressive measures. I identify the resulting state of affairs as just, even though that state of affairs is nothing but the product of the actions and decisions which have brought it into being and sustain it. I cannot do without a shorthand way of speaking here, and since language is partly a response to necessary constraints imposed by realities at all descriptive levels, the use of the term is justified.

## *IV. What About Rights?*

One objection that may be raised against what I have written is that it gives too little space to the subject of rights, a subject which is usually thought to be integral to any plausible theory of justice. I said at the beginning that emancipatory justice is usually expressed in the language of rights, where harmonic talks about responsibilities, but this is only a general characterisation. Otherwise, following Wesley Hohfeld's now standard classification in *Fundamental Legal Conceptions as Applied in Judicial Reasoning* (1923), we may say that human rights, as generally understood, are actually entrenched claim rights, marking the extent to which the emancipatory side thinks it has won a permanent victory; liberty rights also belong on the whole to this camp, as do immunities and individual and group rights. Power rights are the type that belong most obviously to the harmonic party, but as I mentioned a moment ago, this side usually prefers talk of responsibilities. In reality, assigning specific classes of rights to one side or the other is always going to be a hazardous business, as of course is the talk of parties itself. Context, interpretation and caution are paramount here.

The one thing we can always say about rights is that they are more constructs than facts. To the extent that they begin to look like the latter, it might be because they are at the centre of a moral equivalent of WVO Quine's "field of force". But unlike the field that sustains analytic statements, the moral field is always capable of being swept away overnight as by, eg, a natural catastrophe. Once we are back to the *bellum omnium contra omnes*, that is all there is.

## 5. Justice's Dark Matter: Two Puzzles

In this section, I will try to show that our notion of what 'justice' is, is vastly vaguer than we generally suppose. I remarked above that there is a good case to be made for the idea that we derive it from the prior recognition of *in*justice, and that, perhaps this very reason, we are a lot better at discerning injustice.

Ludwig Wittgenstein famously said that if we want to know the meaning of a word, we should look at how it is used. 'Justice', I will argue, has a currency in ordinary language that is not confined to the areas philosophers tend to think it is. A study of *Judge Dredd* and *The Justice League of America* might yield more interesting results than some of the things that are asked of the term in more formal contexts.

Specifically, the conventional notion of justice as fairness might come into question. Although it is possible to treat the two words as synonyms, the word 'fairness' has a much more extensive usage in everyday life. Children's behaviour, for example, is often said to be 'fair', where it would be pompous to call it 'just'. Or one might talk about 'fair play' in a game.

And, of course, fairness is a matter of opinion. It often seems fair when the average movie villain suffers extrajudicial execution at the hands of his victims, even when his or her death is drawn out.

In practice, I think the word 'justice' is a portentous word that tends to be used chiefly in the context of punishment and reparation. I would also contend that the reason we think we can talk straightforwardly about 'just distributions of social goods and offices' is that, because we find ourselves always already within *un*just distributions, we find it difficult to dissociate such talk from notions of *re*-distribution, modes of proceeding, that is, which might have the perceived effect of penalising certain people (say, on Proudhon's premise that property is theft). Of course, we *can* substitute the word 'justice' for 'fairness' in virtually every context (at the aforementioned cost of sounding a little pretentious much of the time, and with the proviso that 'fairness' is a culturally relative term), but why bother when the latter word already does its job perfectly well? And are we not doing something artificial?

Below, I discuss two puzzles connected to the ordinary language usage of justice. Both are 'puzzles' to the extent that we attempt to retain social contract explanations of justice.

## *(a) Kafka's Justice Machine*

Franz Kafka's 1914 short story, *In the Penal Colony*, describes an ingenious machine for dispensing justice. Consisting of three parts, 'the Harrow', 'the Inscriber' and 'the Bed', it first pronounces judgement on whoever is placed inside it (the suspect is always found guilty), then inscribes the sentence into his flesh, then tortures him to death. In what follows, I will call this device Kafka's Justice Machine, although I accept this is not how readers usually refer to it. When Kafka read the story aloud at the Galerie Golz, in Munich in 1916, the audience's reaction was allegedly so extreme, someone fainted.

What is its relevance here? To answer that question, we need to do some preliminary spadework. Kant claimed that whenever I act morally, I am acting on a universalisable maxim. The problem with immoral actions, like lying, he said, is that their universalization results in a contradiction. The very grounds which my ability to make a decision at all presupposes, are undermined.

This is supposedly the problem with all wrongdoing. Kant's formulation of the Categorical Imperative is thus: "Act only in accordance with that maxim through which you can at the same time will that it become a universal law."

Of course, this implies that you *could* choose to act on a destructive maxim, one which, were it to become a universal law, would entail the complete negation of the grounds of your acting thus in the first place. In lying, Kant thinks, I am implicitly acting on such a maxim. And a world in which the institution of promising had no meaning would be one in which I was probably in fear of my life most of the time, since I could no more rely on the state to honour any agreement (however tacit) to preserve my personal safety than I could on anyone else. Similarly, in suicide, according to Kant, I would be willing "a system of nature whose law would destroy life by means of the very same feeling that acts so as to stimulate the furtherance of life".

However, willing a contradiction is absurd, but not necessarily wrong. If I try to make myself a hat that is both green and red all over, or draw a square circle, I am willing something contradictory, but I am not willing something morally wrong. To will something wrong, I would surely have to do something either more, or different in kind.

Arguably, in immoral behaviour, I am willing the absolute destruction of the 'moral law' itself (however circular this might appear). To put it another way, I am willing the contradictory state of affairs (contradictory with my own behaviour here and now) that is the *bellum omnium contra omnes*. I am tacitly willing my own destruction and everyone else's.

If this is correct, then we may happily send any criminal to Kafka's penal colony, because we are merely introducing him to the world he himself has willed. His guilt will always be correctly discovered to be absolute, because his negation of the moral law was always absolute (even if he was only a common or garden liar), and thus the punishment that Kafka's machine inflicts on him will always exactly fit the crime.

Of course, morally speaking, this is grossly counterintuitive, not to say abhorrent. The paradox arises, once again, partly because we are better at identifying injustice than justice. We tend to think the punishment should fit the crime, but if the crime is always – in virtue of its being a crime at all - the willing of the *bellum omnium contra omnes*, and action consistent with that willing, the punishment may invariably be pretty severe, even if we stop short of Kafka's Justice Machine (which we don't have to).

If appeal to Kafka's Justice Machine strikes the reader as a fairly rarefied, it is not. For hundreds of years, most people in Western Europe believed that God had the power, as supreme lawgiver and judge, to consign sinners to burn everlastingly in Hell for such moral transgressions as selling short measures of ale, or for gluttony, or lust. Maybe the majority of sinners would only go to Purgatory and burn for a few hundred years, but still a minority were condemned to eternal torment. However malevolent their actions (and let's concede, for the sake of argument, that at least some of them were exceedingly so), still those actions were limited in space and time. The idea that the just punishment of malefactors can be unlimited in scope is behind the thought-experiment I am proposing here. In any case, it is not so counterintuitive as to deter vast numbers of people from going along with it even, in some parts of the world, today: belief in Hell still being widespread in some communities.

In several ways, *In the Penal Colony* might serve as a metaphor for harmonic justice. Kafka's Justice Machine does not operate in a void. It requires camp guards to oversee and maintain it, and to install the suspects and dispose of the corpses. This whole context exactly mirrors the absolute tyranny that brings the *bellum omnium* definitively to heel, at exactly the point where that tyranny becomes expressible as a form of justice. As I said right at the beginning of this essay, state terrorism only becomes a theory of harmonic *justice* to the extent that the relationship between the implicated parties is expressed in abstract terms (in law courts, or the meetings of tribal elders, for example), and efforts are expended to maintain those relationships in stasis. In Kafka's short story, of course, the Justice Machine is on its way out: it has fallen out of favour with the reigning

Commandant. Harmonic justice is beginning to feel the heat of emancipatory justice, of which the presence of the Explorer there may be one symptom.

The purpose of such reflections here is to show that, once again, we are not clear exactly what justice involves. But more than this. We should by now be a little worried by the connection between justice and morality. This is the issue to which I would now like to turn.

### (b) Justice by Lightning

A boy subjects a girl to an acid attack and leaves the scene smiling. On his way home, he is struck by lightning and dies instantly. In such cases, we might well shake our heads and say that the only positive feature of the whole affair was that justice was eventually done.

This way of talking about justice is quite common. Someone plays a spiteful joke and trips over whilst celebrating; a murderous husband attempts to push his unsuspecting wife off a cliff, but slips and falls to his death; a terrorist buys a faulty bomb which blows him up, leaving everyone around him unharmed. In all these cases, justice is apparently dispensed by an inanimate object.

But this seems to flatly contradict what we said earlier. For we argued there that justice is a matter of decisions.

The odd thing is that inanimate objects do not seem capable of bringing about *in*justices, only justices. If someone performs an act of kindness and is then struck by lightning, all the talk then is of tragedy. We may comment on the injustice of it, but we mean it as a figure of speech (in the same sense we use the phrase 'life is cruel', to mean it is indifferent), whereas I think we actually *do* intend to aver that the lightning strike on the acid attacker really *is* a matter of justice done.

One might suggest that what is really in play here is the historic residue of a religious worldview. Even without knowing it, we are actually attributing responsibility for the outcome to God. It was God's decision to hurl the lightning bolt, etc. Similarly, the religiously-minded might even say it was *literally* an injustice that the kind person was killed by lightning. What we may take from this is that the notion of the dispensation of justice by lightning, or other natural forces, is primitive, and, possibly, one aspect of our most basic instincts for justice.

This may be right, but at best, it only explains the background. Because, the fact is, no matter how atheistic I am, I could still say justice was done when the acid-attacker was struck down. Why? Arguably because one valid understanding of justice is that the victim is compensated-for. The attacker being exterminated by natural forces is one way she might be compensated-for. (I am not suggesting it is the only, or best way, or that she would have to accept it as the sort of compensation she was looking for. It is enough for my purposes that she *might*, and even if she didn't, she might see it as partially compensatory, and that others might too. In any case, we can introduce other accidents into the thought experiment whereby she ends up with more, or different compensation.)

Compensation involves restoring a balance, and thus resorting a prior relative harmony. The fact that we can talk about justice in the acid-attacker case indicates that the notion of harmonic justice plays a part in practical considerations of just outcomes. The 'meta-' level and the normative level in this sort of case are inextricably entangled.

So what now is the connection between justice and morality? For morality requires moral agents. It is not possible for an inanimate object to behave morally. Whereas it *is* apparently possible for one to dispense justice.

This indicates two things.

1. It indicates that the most primitive conception of justice in punishment is harmonic. Harmonic justice is a matter of moving closer to a harmonic state of affairs. What produces the movement doesn't matter. We mentioned earlier that the *bellum omnium* may sometimes be constituted by a war of humans against nature, and that certain forms of harmonic justice may be a way of optimising the body politic to wage that war. In such societies, the natural world would be one real source of injustice and justice alike. As regards our acid-attacker, justice by lightning may be one of those rare instances in which the 'meta-' level of harmony completely commandeers the normative level of morality – just for a moment - and persuades us to adjudge the outcome just.

2. It indicates a radical asymmetry between the notions of justice and injustice. Injustice always proffers someone to blame. Justice does not necessarily proffer anyone to thank: when justice is restored, it is never as a personal favour: even when it is a wholly social phenomenon, it is by an authorised official acting on behalf of the ruling

authority. It is enough that the victim's predicament has been compensated-for. Who or what does the compensating is a matter of broad irrelevance.

This demonstrates again that 'justice' is a derivative term, and that 'injustice' is the older member of the pairing. Justice is a restoration of injustice. When only injustice is present, that is what we call it. As noted above, when only justice is present, we tend to call it something else: 'fairness' or 'social well-being' or 'good government', 'full transparency'. We call something justice when it substitutes one of these four (or their rough equivalents) for a prior situation of injustice. And that appellation lasts only as long as we retain the memory of the injustice it annulled.

As regards the connection between morality and justice, it may help if we borrow the distinction between commanding and commending employed by RM Hare in *The Language of Morals* (1952). That is to say, we should consider 'justice' a commending, rather than a commanding term. Statements of morality, as universal prescriptions, have a commanding character. But commending statements don't have this (obviously this does not mean that justice has nothing to do with ethics, any more than goodness has nothing to do with ethics). Obviously, if something is commended, it has to have first been compared with something less commendable. Once again, we are back to the notion of injustice as primal, and justice as derivative.

## 6. Conclusion

In this essay, I have suggested that we can divide the philosophical inquiry into justice into two parts: a 'meta-' level, which investigates the struggle between two rival conceptions of the term - harmonic and emancipatory - and which is really about what we *call* justice; and a 'normative' level, which asks what justice really *is, in and of itself*. But that the latter investigation is probably best carried out by ethical, rather than political philosophers.

However, I have argued that this recommendation is complicated by the fact that the 'meta-' and the 'normative' spheres of the enquiry are not usually as clear-cut and mutually independent as they are in ethics. In real-life discussions of justice, considerations of harmony and emancipation may often be prominent, if not paramount. Even here, however, the notion of moral good is inevitably vital to grasping the 'real' justice, if any, of the competing claims.

# A NEW APPROACH TO THE PHILOSOPHY OF RELIGION

## Introduction

If one imagines philosophy as a city, then the philosophy of religion is like a museum on the outskirts that hardly anyone visits except on school trips. Step inside and you'll find Gaunilo of Marmoutiers and his lost island, a mock-up of a desert featuring William Paley's pocketwatch, a divided line, and a dog-eared paperback entitled, *Selections from Summa Theologica*. Hardly anything new ever comes in, and the old exhibits are never removed. To the extent that the museum is more than a collection of curiosities, it is a coaching arena, a place for beginners to hone their debating skills before either abandoning the subject altogether, or moving on to do more serious work elsewhere. The museum curators rarely visit any of the more prestigious centres of philosophy – the city-centre vocational institutes – and they rarely, if ever, receive visits in return. And of course, it smells vaguely musty.

In this chapter, I want to propose a new approach to the subject. I argue that the 20th century saw a permanent move from one notion of God (which I shall call the Ptolemaic God, although it isn't necessarily connected to that specific system) to another (what I shall call the Hubble God). This had certain practical as well as theoretic consequences, specifically in religious experience and the connected possibility of ever knowing God. More importantly, I argue that we can no longer expect to produce or discover any chain of reasoning that will provide a definitive answer to the question 'Does God exist?' Rather than asking about God in his *sufficient* characteristics (omniscience, omnipotence, etc. – a fuller list is given below), we can only ask about the *necessary* properties of God, of which I have identified just two: incorporeality and mindedness.

The strength of my position is that it requires philosophers of religion to abandon the museum and move to the city centre. What I am suggesting demands encroachment on the other 'vocational institutes' of philosophy, particularly the philosophy of mind, but also metaphysics and epistemology.

However, in no way do I anticipate that we will be welcomed on arrival. Quite the contrary. And, just to be clear, I regard that as another strength of what I am proposing.

## Of Teapots and Pyramids

Before we begin, it will be as well to get 'Russell's teapot' out of the way. In 1952, Bertrand Russell devised a thought-experiment designed to demonstrate that the burden of proof for those making scientifically unfalsifiable claims lies with those making them.

"If I were to suggest that between the Earth and Mars there is a china teapot revolving about the sun in an elliptical orbit, nobody would be able to disprove my assertion provided I were careful to add that the teapot is too small to be revealed even by our most powerful telescopes. But if I were to go on to say that, since my assertion cannot be disproved, it is intolerable presumption on the part of human reason to doubt it, I should rightly be thought to be talking nonsense."

Which is a fair point, as far as it goes, but unfortunately, the teapot has been put to another use entirely: that of illustrating the absurdity and arbitrariness of the very idea of God. This is roughly the purpose, for example, for which Richard Dawkins employs it in *The God Delusion* (2006). God is no more likely than a celestial teapot, and no more a natural or logical an object of human contemplation.

But a strong argument can be advanced to the effect that the question of God's existence or non-existence is nothing like Russell's teapot. To appreciate why, we have to go back to medieval conceptions of the Great Chain of Being, and arguments like Thomas Aquinas' Fourth Way: the argument for God's existence from degrees of value. Though we no longer credit such conceptions with demonstrating anything real about the universe, the question they raise cannot be so easily set aside. They begin from the fact that that human beings always and everywhere assign grades of value to just about all things: very bad, bad, less worse, satisfactory, good, better, excellent, best.

Humans may not agree entirely on what things to put in what categories, but there is a lot of consensus about the categories. And even, in very general terms, what should go into them. Knowledge is better than ignorance; power is better to possess than impotence; wealth is better than poverty, and so on. Now, for Russell's teapot to be redundant in a discussion about the existence of God, we do not need to think that these ways of classifying the universe represent anything real. Notice however, to begin with, that they combine: it is better to be powerful *and* knowledgeable *and* just, than simply to be knowledgeable, for example. We now have a ladder, a bit like the Great Chain of Being. Or perhaps a pyramid, because the four sides can all ascend to the same place. Suddenly, it is perfectly reasonable to ask whether anything occupies the peak of that construct: is there a being that is omnipotent, omniscient, omnibenevolent, and so on; in other words, a being who combines all the perfections.

Of course, we may well answer 'no'. But the question itself is not only not arbitrary; it is forced on us in the very activity of assigning scalable values to actions, events and objects in the world. It is certainly not absurd, and it is difficult to foresee a time when human beings will ever stop asking it, any more than they will ever stop asking if there is anything over the horizon, or any more knowledge to be had in whatever area. It arises, in short, out of extrapolation. It is therefore nothing like the teapot.

Objections to this include the fact that there are many ways of assigning value to the world. Different peoples and cultures disagree about what is 'perfect'.

But that need not trouble us. In that case, they would disagree about what sort of being lies at the top of the ladder, not about whether there *is* a top (albeit perhaps a vacant one). To say there *couldn't be* a top, a person or culture would either have to claim (i) that there is no such scale bad-good-better-best or (ii) that it is impossible to extrapolate from such a scale. The first objection would probably entail the swift destruction of that culture under forces of natural selection; the second would imply a group of humans who could recognise that A is better than B, but was unable to comprehend the question, 'Isn't C even better than A?'

Another apparent objection might be that virtues inhere in objects. So we have good, better and best kettles, for example, but these have nothing to do with good, better and best wildebeest, and it is difficult to see any peak of a pyramid in which they are united. As Aristotle says, there are as many ways of using the word 'good' as there are ways of using 'is'.

But this objection fails. For 'good' to inhere in an object in the required way, it must be impossible to abstract a set of criteria from the category in which it belongs. Indeed, it might not even be possible to construct such a category in the first place. Besides which, we are not talking about concrete particulars like kettles or wildebeest, but about fundamental ontological properties like extension and knowledge.

This is important point, because when we extrapolate the excellences to perfections, we always find we are talking about some *being*. This is the basis of the Ontological argument as well as Aquinas' Fourth Way: we are talking about God, and (on a highly questionable assumption, ie, that existence is one of the perfections) God must exist. It is also the basis of Ludwig Feuerbach's criticism of religion in *The Essence of Christianity* (1841). The being we are talking about is ourselves, Feuerbach thinks, idealised into a position of ultimate power. In favour of such a position, it has to be admitted that since, in the last two hundred years, we have massively augmented our bodily powers with technology, religion has declined in influence, or at least loosened its grip over the public sphere.

But of course, that does nothing to answer whether the 'thing at the top of the pyramid' exists or not. It simply shows our belief in it fluctuates with circumstances: a social-psychological observation, not a philosophical one.

The point is that both atheists and theists agree in ceding (at the very least, the *prima facie* notion of) the coherence of the *notion* of a top of a pyramid in the sense I have outlined. Otherwise there could be no discussion. It is in this sense that Descartes was undoubtedly correct to say we all possess an *a priori* conception of God. In many ways, once we see that the question of the existence of God is one that is fated permanently to attend the human condition, it becomes one of the most interesting philosophical questions of all. For what could be of more interest than the question of the ultimate being?

## What is God?

Firstly, God would have to be a single being rather than a pantheon, because it would always be possible to ask of the latter, 'Is it possible to combine the individual members' excellences so that they always act fully in concert with shared goals?' But this would be tantamount to saying an improved being would be possess a single mind.

Although they may still possess separate bodies, it could be argued. Under this objection, ten mutually sympathetic, telepathic deities might fit the bill. Until one realises that under another perfection, God has to be omnipresent. There can be no separation of beings within omnipresence because the omnipresent being has to overlap every other being, and if the pantheon already shares a mind, and now fully coincides in extension, any multiplicity it still exhibits is an illusion.

In fact, God's omnipresence might entail something like *panentheism* – the doctrine that God is fully present in all the universe but also above and beyond space and time.

On such a reading of God's omnipresence, we are not talking about the Judaeo-Christian-Islamic God. That God always absent from certain places: sin, for example, excludes him, so does Hell. Indeed, the idea of his absence is implicit in his 'holiness', because 'holy' simply means 'set apart' or 'removed'. The Hindu god would be a better exemplar of this type of omnipresence. In the Upanishads, for example, Brahman, the ultimate spirit, and Atman, the individual soul, are forever one and the same. Mundane reality is *maya*, an illusion, and, by implication, the distinction between good and evil is unsustainable.

However, another reading of God's omnipresence might say that it only entails his being everywhere as an observer, not as a constituent, hence it would not mean that 'geographically' he cannot be where sin is. I will leave the reader to decide whether this is a valid assertion.

God's eternity – his existence throughout all time - should be considered another aspect of his omnipresence, rather than a separate characteristic. We should probably avoid talking about a being who is 'outside space and time' since existence is itself a spatiotemporal phenomenon. There may well be things 'outside space and time' but we have no idea how to conceive them, and thus no idea what the words 'outside space and time' mean in terms of their sense or reference. As far as we humans are concerned, to say something is outside space-time simply means that it is a no-thing: a non-existent.

Luckily, time can be understood in terms of space, which is enough for our purposes. God, if such a being exists, possesses the quality of having been present since the beginning and enduring without diminution to the end. Does he change? Presumably he can have thoughts, because a thoughtless being would not lie at the top of anyone's pyramid. Would he act? He might have the capacity to do so, but whether he would employ it might be another matter. Would he know the future? No necessarily in every detail, because if quantum mechanics is right (or even if it isn't), and there is an element of genuine indeterminism built into the universe, then it might not be possible to know the future. Not knowing it wouldn't necessarily imply a limitation, therefore, any more than not knowing the internal anatomy of a unicorn would.

God's omniscience and his omnipotence complete the list of his qualities. Omnibenevolence, which is sometimes accounted a requirement, is controversial, because, either owing to a prior commitment to the untenability of ethical dualism, as in the Hindu example just mentioned, or because of a need to render God's 'goodness' inscrutable in order to keep the problem of evil at bay, omnibenevolence is not always easy to clarify. Besides which, 'goodness' is open to a variety of interpretations, depending on your era and allegiances.

Now at this point, some readers might wish to stop the discussion in its tracks. There are several well-known paradoxes pertaining to God's qualities, some of them quite ancient. Peter Vardy, in his 1995 *The Puzzle of God*, helpfully lists five:

> "1. If God can do anything, can He commit suicide?
> 2. Can God swim? My six-year-old daughter can swim, so if God cannot do so, this seems a very clear limitation on His power.
> 3. Can God sin? Many of us do this all the time, so if God can do everything, He should be able to do this as well.
> 4. Can God make an object which is too heavy for Him to lift? I can do this with the aid of a concrete mixer, some sand and some cement, but it would seem that whatever answer we give in the case of God necessarily limits His power. If He cannot create such an object, then He cannot do something that a human being can do. But if He can create such a thing, then there is something that He cannot do – namely, lift the object.

5. Can God make an object so that it is completely black all over and at the same time white all over? Alternatively, can God make a square circle?" (p111).

It may be that the notion of an omnipotent being, or an eternal one, involves a logical contradiction. I am not going to argue that it doesn't, but rather that even the apparently undeniable appearance of illogicality is not sufficient warrant for abandoning a discussion about whether God could exist. Because the truth is, we know there exist empirical truths which logic rejects and vice-versa. As an example of the former, consider Zeno's paradoxes, all of which show that space and time do not exist. In a race between Achilles and a tortoise in which the latter is given a head-start, not only will Achilles never catch up with the tortoise, but he can never begin to move at all. Neither can the tortoise. And yet we know that races are run, and won.

As regards an example of a logical truth denied by the empirical world, consider the fact that logically, it ought to be possible to travel at a million miles a second, but science stipulates that the speed of light (186,000 miles per second) is the maximum. Or that it ought to be possible to know the position and momentum of any entity in the universe at a given time, which quantum mechanics denies.

Similarly, it might look to us as if God cannot create an object too heavy for him to lift, and we should bear this in mind as an issue, but we should be foolish to let it forestall our inquiry. If everyone had heeded Zeno, very little science would ever have been done.

# The God of Our Century

The God of the 21st century is arguably a very different being indeed to the God of ancient and medieval times. In those days, God simply had to keep a limited number of planets in orbit around the Earth (or the Sun, if you followed Aristarchus of Samos); the stars weren't that far away and might not even exist as entities distinct from the heavenly firmament. And God didn't have to have been working for very long. Six thousand or so years, according to one estimate. Very difficult work it was, of course, and human beings still have no idea how it might have been begun or accomplished, but nothing in comparison with what he had, and still has, to do nowadays. Recent estimates suggest the universe is at least 13 billion years old, 95 billion light years in diameter, and contains around 500 billion galaxies.

Today, insofar as we have retained the God of the philosophers, we are actually require a completely different conception of that being. Our God is at least 350 trillion cubic light years in size and inconceivably old. To say he could eat Aristotle's Prime Mover for breakfast is an understatement.

It might be objected that we always thought God was infinite in power and extent, so that nothing has changed in this regard. But philosophers have known since the Abbasids that it is impossible to have an actual infinite; only potential infinites exist in the real world (the US Christian philosopher, William Lane Craig has built a plausible defence of the Cosmological argument on this, derived from the work of the eleventh century Muslim thinker, Al-Ghazali). In a finite universe, God's omnipresence will be more or less impressive depending on the size of that universe. In a Ptolemaic universe, or similar, we can just about get our heads round his omnipotence, omniscience and omnipresence; in a Hubble universe, we stand no chance.

This is not a facetious observation, because it means that the top of the pyramid we described earlier is an unimaginable distance above us. Previously, it was thought possible to fit a limited number of beings in between God and humans. The early Christian writer, Pseudo-Dionysius, in *On the Celestial Hierarchy*, lists nine angelic orders in three classes. The Jewish author, Moses Maimonides, lists ten. How many is it possible to fit nowadays?

I said this was not a facetious exercise and I will attempt to demonstrate why. Imagine a disembodied being capable of creating and destroying star-systems at will, whose body is coextensive with the Milky Way (but no bigger). It is kind and loving and its knowledge surpasses ours in a way analogous to that in which ours surpasses that of ants. Thanks to it, we will all eventually be reunited with our loved ones in a trouble-free afterlife, which it – using its knowledge of biology and physics – has set up for us. Among other things, it knows thousands of years in advance when asteroids are on a collision-course with Earth, and it destroys them. It prevents hostile extra-terrestrials from approaching. It wards off countless other dangers arising from yet-to-be-discovered phenomena. Yet it is not omnipotent, nor omniscient. It only prevents the really big catastrophes. He, she, or it, began to exist about two billion years after the Big Bang. It does not know whether there is a being at the top of the pyramid any more than we do. And it is not immortal: it will die, probably in about three billion years' time. Let us call this being God2.

What would be the difference, from our point of view, between God2 and the 'real' God, the God of the philosophers who does (or does not) sit at the apex of the pyramid?

A vain question. One might as well ask an ant to tell the difference between a shed and a skyscraper. The point is, in a universe of the size we inhabit, there is a massive quantity of possible beings completely beyond our comprehension. From God's point of view, God2 is completely insignificant, a cosmic microbe adrift in outer space. But from ours, God2 fulfils everything we might want in a supernatural deity.

This might sound surprising, or counter-intuitive at first. Surely, what we want is a being capable of bringing an end to all evil and suffering. But the fact is, those things are *there*, so the 'real' God either does not exist or is unable or unwilling to end them. God2 cannot, but he can compensate us by giving us a happy afterlife. And he loves us. He does what he can, knowing that – given his limitations and our propensity to misconstrue matters - it is not wise to interfere too much.

In case all this sounds academic, let me draw two practical conclusions.

The first relates to religious experience. No longer is it possible to claim an experience of God with any degree of confidence at all, because of the impossibility of our distinguishing subjectively between God and God2 (and Gods 1.1, 1.2, 1.3, etc. for that matter).

The second relates to the first, and concerns the impossibility of knowing God. Because how could we? What could God do or say that would identify him accurately and uniquely to us, with our relatively infinitesimal minds? What could he show us? Experience and information always requires interpretation, and the only way we could be certain we had interpreted any information about him correctly would be if he was either to take away our freedom in such a way as to enforce recognition, or if he was vastly to increase our cognitive capacities. Arguably, in either scenario, we would no longer be us.

To further underline how far we have moved from the Ptolemaic God, consider Thomas Aquinas' well-known analogical theory of religious language.

The problem of religious language generally can be summed up as the need to explain how it is possible to use human words to refer to and assign sense to superhuman realities. In Christian contexts, for example, it is orthodox to describe God as 'father', but Christians do not mean he is like an actual father. He does not have, nor did he ever have, male genitalia, for example.

Aquinas said words can be used univocally, equivocally or analogically. A univocal term has only one meaning. Equivocal terms have two or more meanings (eg, 'love': think of its use in tennis and in *Four Weddings and a Funeral*). An analogical term is one that applies on different levels: we can talk about a dog loving a human, but dog love can never – so the conventional explanation goes – match human love in terms of depth and complexity. Human love includes elements of pre-cognised long-term commitment and counterfactual obligation that dog love cannot hope to equal. From human love to dog love is an *analogy downwards*. From dog love to human love is an *analogy upwards*.

Now we see where Aquinas is going, because 'love' is also an activity of God. From human-love to God-love is also an analogy upwards. Just as the dog cannot expect to fully understand human love, neither can humans expect to fully understand God's love. But we can at least make *some* sense of it. While 'love' is not used univocally of God and humans, neither is it used equivocally.

Now, notice this works reasonably well with the Ptolemaic God, because it helps us make sense of divine love. Just as the dog's love can be very incompletely mapped onto ours, so our love can be very incompletely mapped onto God's. Our pet dogs understand something of our behaviour towards them, but not everything; likewise, we can understand something of God's love for us, but not everything.

Arguably, however, the whole thing works on a hidden assumption of existential proximity. The more ontologically removed from each other beings are, the more difficult it is to make sense of any application upwards. As regards a being who is, for all practical purposes, infinitely removed from us, it is difficult to see how saying there is an analogy upwards helps. The greater being's 'love' will contain a virtually unlimited number of aspects absent in the lesser being's, and which might completely re-contextualise and revise even supposedly overlapping elements. Such is the effect of what we shall call the Hubble God.

# From Does God Exist to Could God Exist

For a variety of reasons, I do not think we are any longer in a position to ask, Does God exist? in the sense that ancient and medieval thinkers would have recognised the question. Of course, there has always been a tradition within all the major world religions that has denied its legitimacy. God, whatever else he, she or it may be, cannot be *one more object* in the universe, alongside other objects. As Paul Tillich somewhere says: "To affirm the existence of God is as atheistic as to deny it. God is not *a* being, but being itself". Modern writers on the subject, such as Karen Armstrong, have shown how this strand of theological reflection has, by and large, been unjustly neglected by historians. Theistic 'non realism' within all cultures has always had proponents among the spiritually sophisticated.

But I am not arguing for non-realism in that sense. By defining God as the apex of an ontological pyramid, in the tradition of Aquinas, I am committed to treating the subject in a certain realistic sense.

Let me put it another way. Theologians are often keen on telling us that God is 'wholly other'. Taken literally, this would mean that whatever positive statements we can make about ourselves, these should be denied of God. One positive statement we can make about ourselves is that we exist. This would mean God does not exist. Now it may seem like a good idea to say something like this initially, in the heat of philosophical discussion, say, but it is not difficult to see where it takes you. What supporters of this idea really want to say is not that God does not exist, but that he does not 'exist' – ie, not as we know it. The inverted commas are supposed to save the non-realist from the full consequences of his or her denial. We are in the territory of non-cognitive uses of religious language.

But arguably, once you have defined the mode of a thing's existence, you have an excluded middle: the thing either does or doesn't exist. While a thought may not exist in the same way a building exists, and they may both differ from the way in which a quark exists, a thought either does exist *as* a thought or it doesn't, a building either does exist *as* a building or it doesn't, etc. The only exception seems to be Schrödinger's cat, but either way, the cat continues to exist, alive or dead. To go back to Tillich, "being itself" presumably exists.

The idea that God is completely beyond our understanding seems hardly different from saying he is wholly other. Something utterly unknowable is not worth worrying about or even thinking about, and cannot in any case be distinguished within a huge basket of unknowable things like round squares, cubic spheres, borogoves and mome raths, most of which might be quite banal.

One very respectable tradition within Christianity has always grasped this nettle. The negative theology of pseudo-Dionysius the Areopagite proceeds on the assumption that we should only really say of God what he is not. But this includes virtually everything. "He was not. He will not be. He did not come to be. He is not in the midst of becoming. He will not come to be. No. He is not."

I am going to assume that for the purpose of a philosophical discussion about God, we must define God as having at least two necessary knowable characteristics:

God exists incorporeally.

God thinks. Some might say this is implicit in the notion of God's omniscience, but it need not be. It might be possible for a supercomputer to 'know' everything insofar as every time it is asked a question, it outputs a correct answer, and these answers are justified by its other possible answers. But such a computer might be no different to John Searle's "Chinese room", and singularly incapable of thought.

And it is here I think we can make a start. The question "Does God exist?" is about the apex of the pyramid. But the apex of the pyramid is too distant for us to do anything but devise rationalistic arguments about, and as we saw above, what logic supports, the empirical world may reject. In a Hubble universe, the question whether there is a being that simultaneously satisfies the terms 'omnipotent', 'omniscient', 'omnipresent' invites an answer which lies along an almost interminable road with an indefinite number of wrong turns.

At this point, the reader might want to interject. Modern physics, it is often claimed, provides some empirical evidence for the existence of God, depending on how you interpret it, and debarring allegedly incoherent notions of a 'multiverse' (ie, an infinite number of Big Bangs occurring in some unknown medium). The universe is uncannily 'fine-tuned'. For example, it has been calculated that changes in the value of electromagnetism by one part in 10 to the power of 40 would have meant that stars like the sun could never have developed; a change to the force of gravity of one part in 10 to the power of 31 would result in either no creatures bigger than insects being able to develop, or (on the other side) planets being too small for creatures like ourselves to evolve. And so on.

The problem is, even if this argument works, it is no more than a restoration of the teleological argument, utilising physics rather than biology. But David Hume pointed out in the eighteenth century that from a given effect we can only infer a cause sufficient to produce that effect; therefore, to infer a perfect creator, we must assume a perfect universe. But this is a value-judgement about the cosmos we are not in a position to make. In the West, we are accustomed to conflate 'God' and 'the creator of the universe' for obvious reasons, but the creator of the universe need not necessarily be omnipotent, omniscient and omnipresent – much less omnibenevolent. The creator of the universe might still be a God2 type being. (Having said this, Hume's objection is a lot less of a riposte to the Hubble God than the Ptolemaic).

It is not open to us to investigate whether there is an omnipotent being, or even, I have argued, whether omnipotence is a coherent notion. But we can investigate whether it is possible for a being to exist incorporeally and think. To put it another way: is a disembodied mind possible?

In short, the question of the *sufficient* conditions for God's existence is beyond our ability to address. However, we can tackle the question of the *necessary* conditions. If disembodied minds are impossible, God cannot exist.

Notice, this means the subject overlaps strongly with the philosophy of mind. Moreover, it requires us to re-open a question many in that field consider closed.

## Is Disembodied Consciousness Possible?

Insofar as the philosophy of mind is concerned, any suggestion that disembodied consciousness is possible has to begin from a position of what is called *substance dualism*, also sometimes known as *interactionism*. The idea is that there are two substances, mind and brain, that interact.

The modern history of this position begins with the seventeenth century French philosopher, Rene Descartes. Descartes wanted to construct a completely firm foundation for all knowledge, and for this reason, began by asking if there was anything in the World that was immune to doubt. If there was, this would form a secure basis from which to derive any further knowledge. Descartes discovered that any knowledge derived from the senses was capable of being doubted: we might be dreaming, or hallucinating. Admittedly, this is not very likely, but it is sufficient for Descartes' purposes that it is possible.

There was only one thing we could never doubt. The fact that we are doubting. This led to the famous proposition, *Cogito, ergo sum*, I think therefore I am. Since it is possible to doubt my own physical body, the mind must possess one attribute not possessed by the body:

immunity to doubt. Therefore, the mind and the body must be two different things. Hence, dualism.

Descartes was arguing that the mental can be distinguished from the physical on the grounds of certainty, ie, because I can be certain of my own consciousness in a direct manner in which I cannot be certain of anything else. Other arguments for the distinction have been privacy and privileged access - the idea that my mental states are knowable to me in a direct way; to others, they can be known by inference only, if at all.

But in modern times, hardly anyone subscribes to Descartes' argument. Immunity to doubt is not a property intrinsic to the thing itself, but only to someone's perspective. It cannot do the work Descartes wants it to.

And of course, this is far from the only problem with substance dualism. As John Hospers puts it (in considering a mental event - such as volition - causing a physical event - such as a bodily movement),

> "The volition, being a mental event, can hardly touch any physical particles in the brain to give them the appropriate stimulation; but how else can they be caused to move? 'By the mental event' the interactionist says; but the critic who tries to visualize this state of affairs (volition, non-spatial, affecting a spatially locatable part of the brain) finds himself baffled." (*An Introduction to Philosophical Analysis*, p392).

Hospers suggests that this difficulty might be solved by our adopting a wider understanding of causality. Not all causes are physical (eg, magnetism, gravitation, etc). There may be 'action at a distance', and moreover, we sometimes talk of A causing B where we do not know exactly how A causes B, eg, 'smoking causes cancer.' Descartes himself solved the problem by suggesting an area in the brain where the interaction between mind and brain takes place: the pineal gland. Here, he believed, the mind could move what he called the 'animal spirits' - a hypothetical, energy-like fluid which would in turn make the body work. But in the words of one modern commentator,

> "This is no solution at all, of course. For one thing, the problem of interaction is hardly solved by saying that the mind only interacts directly with a part of the brain, since it was not the size of the brain that was the problem. The problem is to show how a massless, sizeless, immaterial mind could have any effect at all on any physical system, large or small. If the mind is adding energy to the system somehow, then it ought to be possible to detect that empirically." (*Philosophy and Artificial Intelligence*, Todd Moody, p30).

The alternative is that the mind is a physical entity: in our (ie, humans') case, the brain. We may contend that a physical, or purely material being could not derive moral or intellectual truths from the World, but in the words of the Buckingham philosopher, Anthony O'Hear,

"What is it about an immaterial substance that enables it to have these insights into generality, necessity and goodness? Here, we are likely to be told Platonic stories about its contact with, or participation in, a superhuman World, but however transcendent this World is, it is still a particular, not itself endowed with or capable of conferring insight into generality and necessity, hard to see as good in itself, apart from some evaluation some being makes of it." (*What Philosophy Is*, p213).

According to O'Hear, substance dualism does not solve any problems about the mind. It simply puts them off.

"Significantly, most of what we are told about [the immaterial self] is what it is not, rather than what it is. We are told that it is immaterial, not what it is made of, that it is connected to the body as a pilot in a ship, but not how it is connected, that it does not decay even apart from the body, but not how it lives or survives. We are not told why or how it gets into contact with a new-born human person, nor how it is motivated to make its choices, except that it is not determined by physical law. We are, in short, told virtually nothing about the operations of this substance, about its relationship to the physical World, or about how it gets into the physical World at all. Moreover, the problematic aspects of human activity - consciousness, rationality, choice, and so on - are all dispatched to the mind, without any further explanation of how the mind does these things. The mind is like an immaterial little man, or homunculus, behind the physical man; it is hard to see how this is not simply a matter of deferring rather than solving the difficulties." (Ibid, p214).

In fairness to interactionism, it might be said that, insofar as all current theories of the relationship between mind and body are hypothetical, they might all be said to be deferring the difficulties: they defer them to a hypothesis which there is currently no way of definitively verifying. What might make the immaterial mind different is that it claims to be unique, and hence by implication, not open to ordinary methods of scientific inquiry. But this may not necessarily be true. Even though one could not necessarily investigate it directly, it might still be susceptible to investigation in virtue of predictable effects - like black holes in space. Thus there is some evidence (which scientists are beginning to take seriously, even if philosophers are not) for the possibility of disembodied consciousness, in Near Death Experiences (NDEs) and Out Of Body Experiences (OOBEs). Scientists do not agree on how such experiences are to be interpreted, but that they could serve as evidence for an immaterial mind, no one disputes.

Despite what he says, O'Hear does appear to agree that the immaterial mind hypothesis might admit of empirical investigation:

"The dualist neurophysiologist, Sir John Eccles, claims to have found evidence for sudden and physically inexplicable brain activity when people will to make certain bodily movements. This is clearly the sort of consequence dualist interactionism would be expected to have, and anyone espousing this view must be prepared to look for this sort of ghostly intervention in the physical world." (p214).

On the face of it, dualism looks to be dead in the water. The problem is that the alternative is materialism (usually called 'physicalism' nowadays, because 'materialism' has unwanted nineteenth century connotations): the idea that there is only one substance to consider: the brain. Materialism's problem is that, rendered consistent, it entails a nasty corollary called epiphenomenalism. Nearly all materialists claim to be able to avoid it, but only with varying degrees of failure.

For this reason, it is likely that in the future, philosophers investigating the necessary conditions of God's existence, as I have identified them, will focus on three areas:

## 1. *Epiphenomenalism*

The problem with thoroughgoing materialism is that it has to be monist: brain events create mental events, but the reverse cannot be true. Otherwise, we are left with a dualist position: if brain events cause mental events, and mental events can have a reciprocal effect, we have interactionism, and it strongly implies, if not entails, that there are two substances that interact. If we have only one substance – matter – causing *qualia* (raw mental feels), intentions, perceptions, memories and thoughts, which have no reverse effect – we have epiphenomenalism. Epiphenomenalism is a daunting position to embrace, because it is so counter-intuitive – a mental decision to raise my arm followed by the physical raising of said limb seems to count against it, for example – and this is why most physicalists manifest what the Rutgers philosopher, Jerry Fodor, called "epiphobia": the fear of turning into an epiphenomenalist.

In this *Matter and Consciousness* (1988), the neurophilosopher Paul Churchland explains the attractions of epiphenomenalism for brain scientists:

> "Put yourself in the shoes of a neuroscientist who is concerned to trace the origins of behaviour back up the motor nerves to the active cells in the motor cortex of the cerebellum, and to trace in turn their activity into inputs from other parts of the brain, and from the various sensory nerves. She finds a thoroughly physical system of awesome structure and delicacy, and much intricate activity, all of it unambiguously chemical or electrical in nature, and she finds no hint at all of any nonphysical inputs of the kind that substance dualism proposes. What is she to think? From the standpoint of her researches, human behaviour is exhaustively a function of the activity of the physical brain. And this opinion is further supported by her confidence that the brain has the behaviour-controlling features it does exactly because those features have been ruthlessly selected for during the brain's long evolutionary history. In sum, the seat of human behaviour appears entirely physical in its constitution, in its origins, and in its internal activities.

On the other hand, our neuroscientist has the testimony of her own introspection to account for as well. She can hardly deny that she has experiences, beliefs, and desires, nor that they are connected in some way with her behaviour. One bargain that can be struck here is to admit the reality of mental properties, as nonphysical properties, but demote them to the status of impotent epiphenomena that have nothing to do with the scientific explanation of human and animal behaviour. This is the position the epiphenomenalist takes, and the reader can now perceive the rationale behind it. It is a bargain struck between the desire to respect a rigorously scientific approach to the explanation of behaviour, and the desire to respect the testimony of introspection." (p11-12).

Churchland coins a 'vague metaphor' to describe epiphenomenalism:

"Think of our conscious mental states as little sparkles of shimmering light that occur on the wrinkled surface of the brain, sparkles which are caused to occur by the physical activity in the brain, but which have no causal effects on the brain in return." (Ibid, p11)

In addition to being counter-intuitive in a way we have already seen, there are obvious problems with epiphenomenalism, which is why so many physicalists are so keen to distance themselves from it. The first might be termed 'the evolutionary argument', and is often associated originally with William James, and more recently with the American anthropologist, Donald Symons. Evolution seems to have occurred in such a way that organisms end up possessing those features that are of broad instrumental value to them. Is it likely that something as significant as consciousness could have emerged from the evolutionary process if it had no instrumental value?

Epiphenomenalists claim to have an answer to this. In *Noises from the Darkroom* (1994), for example, Guy Claxton describes consciousness as a by-product of the brain's increasing power to distribute attention, of no more functional value than the redness of blood or the whiteness of milk.

Perhaps the biggest problem for epiphenomenalism was summed up by John Hospers in 1967.

"The feature that makes epiphenomenalism most difficult to accept is that, since mind never affects body, one is committed to the belief that the entire course of events in the physical World would have been exactly the same as it now is, even if there had been no minds at all. But how, one might ask, could cities have been built, books and symphonies written, colleges attended and courses taught, if human minds were not causally efficacious in the World?" (*An Introduction to Philosophical Analysis*, p397).

If epiphenomenalism is correct, then of course we should have no free will in the traditional sense of my beliefs being able to direct my behaviour. In support of this, monists point to research such as Libet's experiment, which purports to show that we do not have free-will.

To summarise: in the 1980s, Benjamin Libet, a researcher in physiology at the University of California, asked subjects to flick their wrists at random moments while measuring the build-up of electrical activity in their brains. Each subject was placed before a clock and asked to remember the time they made their decision. In each case, Libet was able to show that the build-up of electrical activity began significantly in advance of when the subject was consciously aware of making a choice. Libet's conclusion was that the choice was made first non-consciously, and only subsequently turned into a "conscious decision". Generalised, this could serve as evidence for epiphenomenalism. In effect, the argument against it from counter-intuitiveness fails – I raise my arm because my brain tells me to; the consciousness which apparently motivates the action is, in reality, merely a subsequent side-effect.

And of course, this in turn has generated criticisms. One possibility is that it fails to distinguish consciousness from self-consciousness. I may be conscious of all sorts of things without being reflexively conscious of them. For example, I am certainly conscious when I am driving my car, but ask me to repeat the details of the journey shortly afterwards, and I may well have forgotten them. My consciousness here is a kind of 'rolling consciousness': it occurs then deletes itself. Sometimes, I may need to be self-conscious of my consciousness in order to really appreciate its significance. I see the celebrity in front of me at the supermarket as soon as I join the queue, but I don't *see* her until later.

Others have objected to Libet's experiment on the grounds that finger-moving is a small-scale phenomenon and impossible, as a model, to scale-up to complex decisions like whether I should devote my life to one career in preference to another, whether I should step down as chairman for moral reasons, and so on.

The problem with free will, as all philosophers know, is that it is difficult to pin down. Unless it is to involve randomness (and hence a paradoxical measure of unfreedom), it has to be admixed with a degree of determinism. So that, for example, I am constrained by my moral convictions, my calculations about what is rational, my affections and allegiances, and so on. The payoff is that not to be constrained by these would, for most people, be highly undesirable. For obvious reasons, we call the theory of free-will that is joined to determinism like this *compatibilism*.

But we do not have to worry about this as regards the necessary conditions for a being such as God. The real concern is the recrudescence of epiphenomenalism. But I think we are far from this.

It is worth mentioning that a result like Libet's, in the seventeenth century, might not have been seen as a confirmation of body-first-mind-afterwards theories. Rather, it might have been seen as working in favour of the Occasionalism of Nicolas Malebranche, and thus further evidence for the existence of God. Times change.

## 2. Intentionality

The chief problem with reducing all mental events to physical events was known to the scholastics, but rediscovered for a modern audience at the end of the nineteenth century by the German philosopher and psychologist, Franz Brentano, according to whom:

> "All mental phenomenon are characterised by what the medieval scholastics called the intentional (or mental) grasp of an object, and what we might call, though not entirely clearly, reference to a content, orientation to an object (not to be understood here as meaning a thing), or immanent objectivity. Every mental phenomenon includes something as object within itself ... In presentation something is presented, in judgement something is judged, in love loved, in hate hated, in wanting wanted, and so on. This is a characteristic of mental phenomena exclusively. No physical phenomenon exhibits anything of the sort. We could, therefore, define mental phenomena by saying that they are those phenomena which contain an object intentionally." (*Psychology From an Empirical Standpoint*, 1874)

In short, mental phenomena are always *about* things; to put it another way, they have the property of what some philosophers have called 'aboutness'. By contrast, no physical phenomenon is about anything whatsoever; physical things just *are*. Following Leibniz's universally accepted observation that X is the same as Y if and only if every predicate true of X is also true of Y, it would seem to follow that mental phenomena and brain phenomena must be two different things.

Of course, attempts have been made to get around Brentano by discovering intentionality in other things (sentences, for example, have been held to be non-mental phenomena that are also about things, or information-states). There are three rival materialist explanations of Intentionality: the resemblance analysis, the causal analysis and the levels of explanation analysis.

The resemblance analysis proposes a thing is about another thing if it resembles it. Eg, a map is about a piece of terrain for that reason. This resemblance theory has had notable champions in Aristotle and David Hume. However, whereas resemblance is 'symmetrical', Intentionality is 'asymmetrical': A resembles B implies that B resembles A, but A is about B does not imply that B is about A. Moreover, a thing can be about another thing and not resemble it in any way whatsoever: my paperback *Middlemarch* is about a country village, but it does not resemble one. For these reasons, the resemblance analysis is not very popular among materialists.

The causal analysis says a thing is about another thing if it causes it. Eg, believing that Eric is bearded means that I entertain a brain state caused by Eric's beard. Since Eric's beard causes the brain activity, the latter is about it. The causal analysis has the advantage of asymmetry, but does not account for item number 1 in Brentano's thesis: the belief in non-existent objects. Neither can it really account for misrepresentation. Imagine I take a photograph of Eric, and when it is developed, he looks like a sea-lion. I would say that this misrepresented him, as compared with a photograph in which he looks human. But I cannot say that Eric caused one picture "more" than another. Nor can I talk about "proper" and "improper" causes without making value judgements which defeat the point of materialism.

Thirdly, the 'levels of explanation' analysis says that mental events and brain events stand on different levels of explanatory abstraction. It is common in such cases for B to exhibit different properties to A, even where B and A are the same thing. For the Californian philosopher, John Searle, we are accustomed to think of causation in terms of push and pull – it is natural for us to do this, and it is what underlies the objection to physicalism that reads it as implying epiphenomenalism. But it is a mistaken. Causation involves more than push and pull. In the real world, we have two levels of causal explanation all the time. Thus, my car might be described in terms of pistons, cylinders and spark plugs. But we can also talk in terms of a lower level – electrons, the molecular structure of the metal alloys, the oxidisation of hydrocarbons. The higher level is fully explicable in terms of the lower level, but this does not mean that the higher level is not causally real.

> "It does not prove that the solidity of the piston is epiphenomenal to point out that solidity is explainable in terms of the molecular behaviour of the alloys; similarly, it does not prove that intentions are epiphenomenal to point out that intentions are explainable in terms of neurons, synapses and neurotransmitters." (*Mind, Language and Society*, 1999, p61)

Searle thinks we are asking the wrong question if we ask whether anything can refer intrinsically, as if we can take intentionality and treat it in isolation from the experiences of which it forms a part, and vice-versa. Could we imagine conscious experiences that *weren't* intentional?

> "If we try to treat, for example, our conscious visual experiences as if they were just phenomena in the world like stones or trees or digestion, then it seems a miracle that they could refer. But of course, though they are natural processes, they have a special feature. It is internal to the state that it has this intentionality. It could not be this very visual experience if it was not an experience whose intentionality was that it is a case of seeming to see this thing in front of me." (p97)

This may be just a reiteration of the mystery rather than a solution. We can imagine a complex chemical electrical system producing no intentional states; we can imagine such a system producing high-information energy states with no intentionality (like a television); we can imagine light sensitivity without intentionality. I can even imagine mind without intentionality (if, as thinkers like Guy Claxton believe, consciousness is simply an evolutionary by-product with no causal power, then the mental state causing eating a biscuit, may only be intentional in the very minimal sense of the aforementioned 'causal analysis'). The mystery remains.

More generally, the levels of explanation theory arguably begs the question. If A and B have different properties, more often than not it is because they are different things; in rare cases they are identical, but in those cases, it ought to be possible *in principle* (not usually in practice) to describe B exhaustively in terms of A, and A in terms of B. But no one has the foggiest idea how to translate intentionality into physicalism or vice-versa.

It is possible to ask an interesting question about levels. Given that (1) the lowest level of mind, on a physicalist definition, must be elementary particles – superstrings, or quarks and leptons, and these are 'immaterial' in the classical sense; and (2) the highest level of mind is electrical activity produced by neurons, then (3) we are always running from energy to energy. Ordinary matter – ie, the brain – is an intermediate through which the process is enabled. But is it necessary? Functionalists will maybe say no, but even they are then committed to the idea that there must be some other material intermediary. Are they correct? This is of course, a highly speculative question, and we are nowhere near the point where it would be possible to answer it with the slightest confidence (the second law of thermodynamics would seem to stand firmly in its way, but arguably of all complexity here), yet it is part of the job of philosophy to ask questions even where answers are impossible. Something like Leibniz's metaphysics, suitably revised (the EPR paradox, after Einstein's 1935 paper discussing two particles travelling away from each other at light-speed, seems at least compatible with his monadology), might address it.

The problem of intentionality comes into its sharpest relief when it encloses highly abstract procedures.

Imagine I am doing a lengthy and difficult mental calculation in advanced mathematics. It is questionable whether anything in the brain could ever allow the specific steps of that computation to be read off by an observer who was given unlimited access to the brain but no further clue as to what its owner was doing (or equally, produced by a scientist given unlimited power to chemically-electrically manipulate a person's brain tissue). The 'aboutness' here is inaccessible from outside.

## 3. Near Death Experiences

Philosophers and scientists tend to hate mention of out-of-body and near-death experiences, because all such phenomena have a strong whiff of the occult. Taking them too seriously therefore invites ridicule, contempt and the withdrawal of the good will of academia. In my previous book, *21st Century Philosophy*, in the context of the Sokal affair, I discussed the possibility that the academy might be, in one of its aspects, skewing the intellectual production of the west. I will not repeat that discussion here; suffice it to say that 'the paranormal' is now something no one in universities wants to be too closely associated with. One cannot even imagine the sort of thought-provoking work Sylvan Muldoon and Hereward Carrington produced in the nineteen twenties, and neither of these men was an academic by profession. The closest such figure today is the estimable Susan Blackmore, and although she left her academic post (in 2001) a convinced sceptic, at least she considered the paranormal a fit area of rigorous study. Even she spoke of having to work "without grants and usually without a job" (*The Guardian*, January 12 2010).

There is now fairly substantial body of empirical evidence for Out Of Body Experiences (OOBEs) and Near Death Experiences (NDEs). We may need to give the reader a flavour of the sort of thing under discussion. Since a Near Death Experience typically involves an OOBE, we will describe a typical NDE (in the first person for the sake of added realism).

> "I was lying on the operating table, and I heard the doctors pronounce me dead. My husband, who was present, was told to come back in the morning, to collect my death certificate. The strange thing was, that I did not seem to be dead at all! I had, as it were, 'floated' up to the ceiling, and I could see everything that was happening. I wanted to tell the people below that it was all right, I wasn't dead. The next thing I knew, I was in a long, dark tunnel with a brilliant light at the end - so bright it seemed to be brighter than the sun. I was travelling along this tunnel, towards the light. When I got to the end, I was met by an old man who I knew was my grandad - he had died several years earlier. He seemed to be prompting me to a decision, to go forward into an indescribable joy or go back. I remember saying, 'Well, if I died, who would look after the baby?' The next thing I knew, I awoke in the operating theatre. Someone was excitedly saying, 'Sister, we've got a pulse!'"

The OOBE begins and ends with the floating above the physical body in the operating theatre. The NDE begins with the entrance to the long, dark tunnel. It should be sufficient to prove that an OOBE occurred to show that disembodied consciousness is possible, and that the above dismissals of disembodied existence - all of which are made from a rationalist standpoint - are defunct. Such proof has yet to be provided.

In 1975, the American scholar, Raymond A. Moody, published his bestselling *Life After Life* (Bantam Books). Moody had doctorates in philosophy and medicine, so was fairly uniquely positioned to be able to examine the evidence. His book contained interviews with patients who had clinically 'died' but were resuscitated. Moody's claim was that NDEs might give us insight into what happens after death, and he put forward a list of features of the typical NDE which is still influential on researchers in the subject today.

In the early 1980s, Michael Sabom, an American Cardiologist, attempted to debunk Moody's credulous approach to OOBEs. He believed that he would be able to show that what people said they saw from their 'floating' position was, in each case, a mental reconstruction of facts that were available to them (even if they were unconscious) during the time of their resuscitation. For example, they might have unconsciously heard the words 'Come back in the morning and collect her death certificate', and the brain may have somehow 'converted' these words into a mental image, persuading the subject that she actually *saw* the event taking place, when in reality, it was little more than a special type of dream. With this end in mind, Sabom taped interviews with one hundred people who had had OOBEs after heart attacks. He also looked up each patient's hospital file, where the specific details of how they had been resuscitated had been recorded. His conclusion was surprising, not least to himself. He found that most people were able to give specific, unique features of their own resuscitation, which were not discussed at the time and were out of the subject's visual field. In many cases, the features were too unique to have been 'reconstructions' based, eg, on prior watching of TV resuscitation cases. Sabom collected his researches in *Recollections of Death: A Medical Investigation* (New York 1982) and concluded, "In each case, I have been able to show that there was a wide agreement between what they said they saw happen and what really did happen."

There are a large number of sceptics, of course, and they tend to claim that all NDEs are similar because we all have similar brains. This has the benefit of respecting Ockham's Razor, the notion that, of two competing explanations of equivalent power, the simplest should be preferred for practical purposes. Obviously, it is simpler to assume a brain than a brain and a mind. In *Focus* magazine in 1994*, Susan Blackmore explained the NDE thus:

> "In fact, tunnel experiences, far from being confined to the edge of life, occur with hallucinogenic drugs, in ecstatic states and just before sleep. The common feature in all these is not the proximity of death, but excess activity in the visual cortex - the part of the brain that processes visual information.
> In the brain, neurons interact by sending chemical signals across fine gaps, called synapses. The effect either excites or inhibits the next cell. Inhibition serves to keep levels of brain activity 'damped down' and is

largely the process responsible for stabilising brain activity.

Studies of rat brains show that in an oxygen shortage, inhibitory signals disappear before excitatory ones do, so inhibition is less effective and the cells fire randomly. What would this look like to the person whose brain it is?

The answer depends on understanding the relationship between the visual scene as it appears on the retina at the back of the eye, and the same scene represented in the visual cortex of the brain. This mapping from one to the other is well understood. There are lots of brain cells devoted to the centre of the visual field (where you look directly) but very few to the edges. If the cells start firing randomly there will be more in the middle, fading to the outside and giving the impression of a tunnel.

A computer can be programmed with information about this mapping to simulate the effect of excess activity. The result is very much like a tunnel - bright light in the middle, fading out becoming darker and darker at the edges; if the level of activity increases, the central light seems to get closer, as if you are travelling along a tunnel."

The Out of Body experience is equally explicable in terms of brain activity.

"The psychological view is that the brain builds models of or representations of the World - rather than directly perceiving it 'as it is' ... For obvious reasons this model of the World is usually constructed from an eye-level view, as though there is someone inside your head looking out through the eyes. But what happens when the brain is failing, when there is not enough neuronal input from the eyes, or when the system is confused by pain, fear and stress? Presumably, the brain will still keep building models of the world, but they will have to come from the imagination and memory, and not from the senses.

So what would such models be like? If they are anything like dreams and recollections, they could well be seen in a bird's eye view. And if this is the best model the system can construct at the time, it will seem as real as anything ever seems."

These are good explanations, though they do (as should be expected in an area like this) leave some unanswered questions. To begin with, in many NDEs, subjects report reaching the end of the tunnel with undiminished clarity; but this is precisely what they cannot do, if the computer model is accurate. Another problem is that dreams and recollections are not normally seen from a bird's-eye view.

Recent discussion of the subject of subject has hinged on when the experiences happen. If they occur just as the subject is entering or leaving unconsciousness, they may admit of a naturalistic explanation, since one feature of dreams and hallucinations is apparent time-distortion: what seems, to the subject, like a long time, can in reality be very brief.

# Final Observations

In this essay, I have argued that it is no longer possible to argue for God's existence in the traditional sense. This is not a controversial thesis, and philosophers of all stripes will most likely accept it. Less likely to gain a sympathetic hearing is my contention that there is a distinction to be made between what I have called the 'Ptolemaic God' and the 'Hubble God', that the former has been permanently replaced by the latter, and that this has meant we can at best focus, philosophically, on investigating the necessary conditions of Godhead, not the sufficient.

I have tried to show that certain areas within the philosophy of mind should be of particular interest to philosophers of religion, but I hope this will not be misunderstood as advocating that such philosophers should defend substance dualism, much less take up cudgels on its behalf. Philosophy is philosophy and it is best practised when it is not attached to an agenda.

Of course, if it turns out that the human consciousness is explicable entirely in physical terms, this will not necessarily mean that there is no disembodied consciousness anywhere in the universe (though it will reduce the likelihood). If it turns out that disembodied consciousness is possible, neither will that entail God's existence. We are talking about minimal conditions here.

One consequence a valid philosophical argument for disembodied consciousness might have is to make people think about what it is humans really want from a God. I suspect it is a being who is worthy of worship, rather than one who fulfils all the classical philosophers' criteria – omniscience and omnipotence and so on. I suspect we have been led astray by these latter, and that if God2 existed, we would feel it appropriate to worship that being, rather than reserve our allegiance exclusively for some inconceivably distant entity who resides at the pyramid's apex.

--------------------

FOOTNOTE: * I have kept the transcript of this, but not the source, so I know these are Dr Blackmore's words. *Focus* magazine 1994 is an educated guess based on memory, but my apologies to both parties if it is a mistaken attribution.

# ON THE POSSIBLE VARIETIES OF CONSCIOUSNESS

In this chapter, I address the question of how we go about ascribing degrees of mindedness to things we discover in the world. I argue that we proceed by means of two classes of data and a hermeneutic. The two data classes are: (1) the size and complexity of the individual's nervous system and (2) the individual's behaviour. These are processed by a hermeneutic that gives overwhelming precedence to (2), and which states, roughly, that species generally seek to survive, and to preserve and transmit their genetic material. For scientists, questions of mindedness play no part in this reckoning. They can afford to be agnostic on the matter. For philosophers, it is a different matter.

I further argue that, owing to the problem of missing senses, one of the key components of this calculation – (2) – is radically unreliable. This only leaves (1) as a means of determining the degree of mindedness of an individual. (1) fails in the same way that the argument for other minds from analogy fails. On a planet containing 8.7 million species, we only really have access to the human mind, and although we know this accompanies a very complex nervous system, we cannot covert this to a more generally applicable conclusion. For all we know, there may be higher consciousnesses in other species with much more rudimentary 'brains' than ours – consciousnesses of a type we are necessarily unable to conceive.

## Kinds of Minds

How many categories of mind are there in the world? This looks like a difficult question, but luckily someone has already been there. In his *Kinds of Minds* (1997), Daniel Dennett suggests a fourfold taxonomy, inhabiting a metaphorical 'Tower of Generate and Test'. On the bottom are Darwinian creatures whose responses to their environment are simple and inflexible; on the next level up are 'Skinnerian' creatures that can react to adverse stimuli in a series of ways until they reach a favourable outcome; then come 'Popperian' creatures. These have the capacity to represent their environment mentally, and can make a correct initial response to an adverse stimulus, based on a kind of cognitive modelling. Finally, there are the 'Gregorian' creatures – creatures like ourselves. These use mind tools – principally language – to mould their environment. They are named after the British psychologist, Richard Gregory, who came up with the idea of 'kinetic intelligence': what Dennett calls 'smart moves'.

Behind this is probably the 'dimmer switch' notion of consciousness, popularised by writers like Susan Greenfield, only applied across species. Ants have very little, if any consciousness, mice more, dogs even more, chimpanzees still more, and humans most of all. On this understanding, it is possible to draw a picture analogous to Rudolph Zallinger's famous 'March of Progress' where a homo sapiens marches from left to right trailing his evolutionary forebears in strict developmental order.

In the analogous picture – we'll call it 'March of Mindedness' - homo sapiens would trail grades of non-human organism, from primates, through mammals, reptiles, insects, all the way down - on the picture's far left - to single-celled creatures and plants. The great chain of being, minus its supernatural occupants: an uncanny secular scientific validation of Genesis 1.

In 1997, Channel 4 aired a one-hour investigation into animal consciousness under the title, *Do Vampire Bats Have Friends?* Among other things, it featured ravens discovering novel ways of obtaining food, a parrot apparently distinguishing shape and colour, monkeys with social skills and bats sharing meals with non-relatives in the seeming hope of the favour being reciprocated someday. The film was divided into sections, one early one of which was called 'They *might* be robots', introduced by Cecilia Heyes of University College London. She said:

> "The problem is that, as most of us understand self-awareness, we only have one case to go on: our own. We know for sure – I know for sure – that I am conscious. Now, when you have that sort of view of what consciousness is, as something intrinsically private, then really it's the case that you can't know for sure whether any other creature is conscious. So the possibility arises that they're *not*; that they're all little robots; behaving cleverly, but with no internal light on, as it were. If a creature is not conscious as we normally understand consciousness - as a private thing – then it's something like a sleepwalker, or as we conventionally understand an automaton or a robot to

be. And it's conceivable, it seems to me, that animals are like that. That doesn't mean we should assume they are."

Consciousness may or may not be a private thing, depending on whether you follow Wittgenstein and Gilbert Ryle. But this is not a bad starting point and it suggests that we should begin by considering the philosophical problem of other minds.

## The Problem of Other Minds

The problem of other minds may be summed up in a single question: how can I ever know that anyone else is having experiences such as mine, or indeed has a mind at all, since I can never have direct access to anyone's mind but my own?

Imagine another possible world, in which, when you are stabbed, I feel the pain, but you feel nothing, and vice-versa. In this case, I am still not feeling your pain, and you are not feeling mine. If I feel the pain, it is my pain, regardless of where the injury is.

So I do not know that you are having a pain: I infer it. But normally, when I infer something, it is possible for me to test the inference – maybe not right away, but sometime. For example, I think I smell burning; I infer that my toast is on fire, so I check the grill. But I cannot check the validity of my inference that you have a pain.

It is even possible to go beyond this, and ask the question, how do I know you have any feelings *at all*, let alone that you are experiencing pain? From my perspective, you might be a robot (the problem with Dr Heyes's position is how to stop scepticism overflowing like this), cleverly programmed to behave like a human, but actually experiencing nothing at all. Indeed, how do I know that *everyone* is not a robot? The fact that you can produce the symptoms of pain does not necessarily prove anything at all beyond the bare fact that you can produce the symptoms of pain.

At first glance, this may seem like a pointless problem, just a trivial sub-question within the broader realm of a philosophical scepticism that asks how we can ever know *anything at all* with certitude. For what it is worth, I think it is insoluble. Its interest here lies in the canonical 'solutions', because these give us some insight of where and why we attribute mindedness. The insight flows not from the success of these answers (as I have just said, I think their failure is inevitable), but from what they reveal in terms of hidden assumptions concerning our everyday attributions of mindedness.

## *1. Behaviourism*

A first attempt at a solution to the problem comes from Behaviourism. This is generally thought to be a psychological theory, but it has a philosophical counterpart, associated with Gilbert Ryle's 1949, *The Concept of Mind*. Ryle's thesis is that when we speak of an action done, for example, intelligently or with sensitivity, we are not suggesting that the act is preceded or initiated by some mental fact, such as intelligence or sensitivity, but rather that the actions meet with certain agreed *standards* of intelligence or sensitivity, or that they were not imposed on the actor from outside. The mind is not a thing; predicates used of the mind refer not to some 'inner' state, but to a person's behavioural dispositions, or to descriptions we might give that person's behaviour. Thus, if we say that I 'know' how to fly a jet, we are not saying that there is something latent in my mind that can at all times and places be identified as this knowledge; what we are saying is that given a jet, a runway, access to the cockpit, and all the other appropriate conditions, I will successfully fly a jet.

With both Ryle and the psychological behaviourists, there is a strong feeling that to talk of someone's beliefs, knowledge or any other mental state, is pointless, since it does not explain what they do. For example, if I say someone has a belief, I am saying that they will behave in such-and-such a way under given conditions. To say that they *will* do so, does not explain *why* they do so, but neither does saying they have the belief, or mental state.

A problem with the behaviourist thesis might seem to be the question of what I mean when I say, eg, 'I am happy'. I would verify 'I am happy' differently to the way in which I would verify 'you are happy'. But this problem can be solved by seeing 'I am happy' not as a statement at all, but rather, as the way in which other people have, on the basis of my behaviour in infancy, taught me to express my happiness. Thus, the apparent difference between first and third person statements can be overcome, as Norman Malcom, the American philosopher, suggests, 'by virtue of their being tied, in different ways, to the same behavioural criteria.' In *An Introduction to Metaphysics*, 1950, CH Whiteley makes the point that,

"It is not very plausible to say that I first become aware of anger in myself, and come to believe in the anger of other people by analogical reasoning. A child is probably aware of the anger of its parents as something to be afraid of, long before she is capable of discovering the analogy between their anger and her own, which feels to her quite different." (p88)

Behaviourism gets rid of the problem of other minds, because it reduces the concept of mind to observable behaviour. Mind is behaviour, and since we can verify empirically that there is behaviour, there must be mind. Thus, Behaviourism doesn't so much *solve* the problem of other minds as *dissolve* it. It denies that there is a problem to be addressed.

## 2. Mentalistic Words as Public Phenomena

According to this solution, the possibility of my applying mentalistic words like 'hope', 'pain', 'joy', 'curiosity', etc., to myself means that, by inference, I already accept a belief in other minds. For where do I learn the meaning of such words? Well, not by looking inside my head and finding some emotion that I pick out and call (say) 'curiosity'. On the contrary, I learn how to use these words by noticing how others apply them, both appropriately and inappropriately. I then take what I've learnt and, in applying the words to myself, I try to imitate society at large by applying the public criteria successfully. All talk about 'the problem of other minds' ignores this. It rests on the false assumption that I find the mentalistic phenomena first in myself, so that I can then ask questions about others, and whether they feel as I do. But this puts the cart before the horse. The question about whether *I* feel curious isn't really a question about 'what's going on in my head': it's a question about whether I'm using the word appropriately or not (and this has hardly anything to do with what's going on in my head). The other minds 'problem' is thus a non-problem. 'Minds' means 'mental states' – things like happiness, joy, ruefulness, etc, and these things are publicly defined.

## 3. *The Argument from Analogy*

The argument from analogy is associated with Bertrand Russell and John Stuart Mill. This states that others are like me in body (including brain and nervous system) and behaviour; since I know that I am minded, and since others are outwardly so much like me, I am entitled to infer that they too are minded. This inference would be partly justified by the fact that it allows me to predict someone's behaviour with a fair degree of accuracy on most occasions. I ask myself what I would do in their position; given that they (usually) do it, this persuades me that they are minded, because I correctly predicted their behaviour by means of an appeal to my own mindedness. And I know I am minded.

## 4. *Criteriological Accounts of Mind*

This 'solution' to the problem of other minds claims that something has a mind is just to say that it fulfils certain limited objective criteria. The test proposed by Alan Turing (the 'Turing Test') which would allow us to say whether a computer is minded, yields a criteriological account of mind. If an entity can pass the Turing Test, so the dogma goes, we know everything we need to know about it to state that it is minded, and no other question is relevant.

## 5. *The Inference to the Best Explanation*

Philosophers nowadays are most likely to want to solve the problem of other minds using an inference to the best explanation. Faced with a person who is crying in pain after stubbing his toe on a video-cabinet, we may put forward two possible explanations to account for his crying. Either he is crying for the same reason I would cry – that is, the pain is too intense; or he is crying because he is an automaton who, for reasons unknown, very strongly resembles me.

The second explanation is likely to 'multiply entities needlessly', and thus involves a violation of Ockham's Razor, the philosophical principle that says the best explanation, chosen from amongst one or more possible explanations, each with equal explanatory power, is the simplest. Of course, the second explanation *could* be simpler (since we are dealing with 'reasons unknown'), but we can probably imagine a greater number of ways in which it is the opposite. So we should probably prefer the first.

We ordinarily define knowledge to include what can be inferred. If we were simply to define knowledge as what we experienced, we would have to say that we have hardly any knowledge at all.

## *How Many Different Solutions Are There?*

The astute reader may have noticed that (2), (3) and (4) are all, arguably, versions of (1), and (5) is a version of (3).

In (2), applying the concepts to others is linked to observing their behaviour; in (3), I do not normally look at the brain and nervous system of another person, so I am limited to drawing my analogy on the basis of body and behaviour – behaviourism again; and in (4), the criteria usually turn out to be behavioural – in the Turing Test, where outputting sentences is a type of behaviour.

As regards (5), one can only conclude that he is in pain because I would be in pain, and he is like me. But this dissolves (5) into (3), and we have already seen that (3) implies behaviourism (1). It looks as if (3) analogy, and (1) behaviour, are more foundational in terms of the explanations we do use in practice to 'solve' (without ever solving it philosophically) the problem of other minds.

We may conclude by noting that we probably ascribe other minds by means of behaviour, and analogy widely interpreted: this would include - in creatures too dissimilar to us in bodily parts - observation of the behaviour of brain and nervous system. Note that we cannot identify something as a brain until we have seen it behave in certain ways analogous to ours: a brain that exhibits no behaviour at all, ever, cannot be accounted such on purely structural grounds. Brain and behaviour are conceptually separate, however, so let us separate them for the sake of argument. In this essay, I have used the word 'brain' rather loosely to mean total nervous system, sometimes even where no central organ present.

So how do I know whether a gnat is minded? I look at (1) its behaviour and (2) the complexity of its nervous system and I apply (3) a hermeneutic, H, stipulated by a modern version of Darwinism, according to which a species' primary purpose is the transmission of its genetic material. H includes assumptions about what counts as rational within a creature's world. It makes a series of methodological assumptions, in other words, whose strength is that they supposedly apply across the whole of biology. (It is not open to me as a gnat-researcher to break away from them, even if that were possible.) We might describe the brain/ nervous stem complexity and the outward behaviour as the raw data, H as the formula or data processor into which they are entered, and the result yielded as lying somewhere on a continuum from 1 (human consciousness) to 0 (inanimateness).

It is not so much that I find the gnat is *not* minded: I can afford to remain agnostic about that, because I never need to give a total explanation of the gnat. My job is to provide a description of its behaviour consistent with H. That is all. If I were to be *asked* to assess whether it is minded, I can reasonably answer, like Laplace, 'Sir, I have no need of that hypothesis'. It may be that we have a parallel here to what has happened in psychology, where working assumptions that mind and brain are identical have given rise, over time, to a 'fact' to that effect. And the exclusion of questions of mindedness from entomology, oligochaetology, etc., has given rise to the 'fact' that the relevant creatures lack minds. If this fact has a justification at all, it is to do with the relative complexity (or lack of it) of the nervous system; it cannot be to do with behaviour, as I hope to show later. But I do not believe relative complexity of nervous systems is a sufficient warrant for such far-reaching conclusions. It falls down partly for the same reason the solution to the problem of other minds from analogy fails: we only have our own species to go on. And given that there are 8.7 million species in the world, that is too slender a basis.

## Missing Senses

In Book 2, Chapter XII of his *Essays* ('Apology for Raimond Sebond'), the sixteenth century French thinker, Michel de Montaigne, addresses the subject of missing senses. Now, of course we all know today that humans possess more than the five senses discussed by Aristotle in *De Anima* – for example, proprioception and the ability to distinguish heat and cold, but I do not think this undermines Montaigne's basic point. He writes:

> "The senses are the beginning and the end of human knowledge ... I make a doubt whether or no man be furnished with all natural senses. I see several animals who live an entire and perfect life, some without sight, others without hearing; who knows whether to us also one, two, three, or many other senses may not be wanting? For if any one be wanting, our examination cannot discover the defect. It is the privilege of the senses to be the utmost limit of our discovery; there is nothing beyond them that can assist us in exploration, not so much as one sense in the discovery of another.

'Can ears the eyes, the touch the ears, correct? / Or is that touch by tasting to be checked? / Or the other senses, shall the nose or eyes/ Confute in their peculiar faculties?'"

If we *were* missing any senses, we would no more be able to discern the fact than a man born blind would be able to discern his lack of sight.

"It is impossible to make a man naturally blind conceive that he does not see; impossible to make him desire sight, or to regret his defect; for which reason we ought not to derive any assurance from the soul's being contented and satisfied with those we have; considering that it cannot be sensible herein of its infirmity and imperfection, if there be any such thing."

Now, as I mentioned, we nowadays accept that the number of senses humans possess depends on your method of counting: you can group them in such a way as to bring the number in under five, partly depending on what you think a 'sense' is. Some scientists suggest three: mechanical, chemical and light. Some say you cannot separate them: they work in conjunction. But, as I have already stated, I think Montaigne's basic point remains. Let me say why.

Firstly, we can all imagine ways of perceiving things that are at present imperceptible. For example, when I read a comic about a masked crusader with superpowers, I imagine such a thing without the slightest effort. But I can also imagine that our senses might have evolved differently. Our eyes might have been equipped with interchangeable lenses that allowed us to see and recognise the very small (so we could avoid harmful bacteria, for example), or our ears might have evolved a higher frequency switch, or we might have developed the olfactory capacities of a dog.

But we don't *need* such things, the reader will protest. And that is precisely my point. Evolution is quite stingy. It gives us what we need to navigate the part of the world we inhabit so as to ensure our survival. The reason why moles cannot see, nor cephalopods hear, nor vultures smell, is that they do not need to. To thrive as species, they only need to access the world in certain ways. They have missing senses, but they do not miss them. And while we are on the subject, we should not delude ourselves into thinking we are necessarily at the top of the evolutionary tree: Christopher's Lloyd's *What on Earth Evolved? 100 Species That Changed the World* (2009), for example, ranks humans sixth, behind earthworms, algae and cyanobacteria. Not that it matters. It would be facile to assume a straightforward correlation between insight into total reality and material success, otherwise, philosophers and theoretical physicists would all live in much bigger houses than hedge-fund managers and investment bankers. They would also mate more frequently.

Part of the issue here is that, if species are only given the senses sufficient for survival, these may not be sufficient for a very different task: that of generating a complete understanding of the whole world, a genuine 'view from nowhere'. Montaigne's point stands. And H may be the only hermeneutic creatures like us can ever get.

## Parallel Universes/ Possible Worlds/ Extra Dimensions

Is it possible that the world we think we know through science is effectively just a part of reality, the remainder being 'closed off' to us in one or more of its aspects? As Montaigne says, no empirical investigation could answer this question, but a rationalist one – making use solely of the apparatus of reason alone – might. Something like Zeno's paradoxes or Kant's antinomies could conceivably reveal that there is something slightly wanting in a predominantly *a posteriori* interpretation of the world.

And arguably, this is what we find. Obviously, parallel universes, possible worlds and extra dimensions are not equivalent terms, often even where the same term is used by different writers. They have in common a conception of other places inaccessible to us by any ordinary means, or more often, any means at all. It seems many respectable philosophers and scientists believe there must be such things. Of course, they disagree about how to describe them.

Physicists like to talk about different dimensions, or a multiverse, or parallel worlds. Some of these are mathematical constructs, not empirical realities, but not all. According to *ScienceDaily*, 30 October 2014:

"In a paper published in the journal Physical Review X, Professor Howard Wiseman and Dr Michael Hall from Griffith's Centre for Quantum Dynamics, and Dr Dirk-Andre Deckert from the University of California, take interacting parallel worlds out of the realm of science fiction and into that of hard science.

The team proposes that parallel universes really exist, and that they interact. That is, rather than evolving independently, nearby worlds influence one another by a subtle force of repulsion. They show that such an interaction could explain everything that is bizarre about quantum mechanics.

Professor Wiseman and his colleagues propose that:

• The universe we experience is just one of a gigantic number of worlds. Some are almost identical to ours while most are very different;

• All of these worlds are equally real, exist continuously through time, and possess precisely defined properties;

• All quantum phenomena arise from a universal force of repulsion between 'nearby' (i.e. similar) worlds which tends to make them more dissimilar."

And this comes long after David Lewis, who in 1973 published *Counterfactuals*, arguing that possible worlds are concretely real. Despite widespread incredulity at the time, he was recently voted the thirteenth greatest philosopher of the past two hundred years (on the *Leiter Reports* website, run by the Chicago university professor, Brian Leiter).

The best-known contemporary representative of this tendency is perhaps the physicist, Max Tegmark, who says that all computable mathematical structures really exist: the so-called Mathematical Universe Hypothesis (MUH).

Now this is all well and good, many readers will now be saying, but what does it have to do with the section on missing senses? Surely, there is no suggestion that there are minds on earth with missing senses that enable them to access these dimensions?

I think it is a possibility, but no more. One may even construct an argument to the effect that human beings themselves possess this capacity in part. Let me explain.

One theory of parallel universes says that there are an infinite number of such things. Whatever I can imagine is a possible world, and unless it conflicts with the laws of logic, or mathematics, or (in some versions) physics, it is a concrete reality somewhere.

Now, I can imagine that there exists a possible world in which I my eldest son is a bearded all-in wrestler. According to the theory, however much of an affront it may appear to common sense, such a universe exists somewhere. Therefore, when I form a mental picture of my son as a bearded all-in wrestler, I have *knowledge* of him as such. After all, what is it to have knowledge of a thing? As I write this, my Kerry Blue Terrier sits next to me on the sofa. I know that because light enters my retina and is resolved in my brain into an image which I consider (if I consider it at all) veridical. It is the mental image which constitutes the knowledge. I assume it relates to an equivalent entity 'out there' – on the sofa in this case.

When I imagine my son as a wrestler, I also have a mental image, and if the theory is true, I am completely justified in thinking it corresponds to a reality 'out there' (although hopefully not on the sofa). In short, I have *justified true belief*, which is the very essence of knowledge.

Now some readers will argue that this ignores the Gettier problem: that justified true belief does not count as knowledge where the belief arises for invalid reasons. But Gettier's problem only applies if the theory that there exists an infinite number of parallel universes in which every possibility is realised, is false, or if the scientists / philosophers who have deduced it are right, but for the wrong reasons. Otherwise, Gettier does not apply.

But it might not apply in any case. Gettier's problem may only apply to propositional knowledge. Arguably, what is under consideration here is something more akin to knowledge by acquaintance – insofar as my knowledge is constituted in and by the mental image, not by assent to a sentence.

If this argument is true, imagination might count as a sixth sense, a very dim one. In another creature, it might permit genuine access. Note that nothing in the theory itself, or in physics, mathematics, or logic, could definitively preclude such a possibility.

And of course, ultimately, we are not really talking about imagination, rather some faculty analogous to it.

Perhaps it will be objected that no certain meaning can be given to 'analogous to' here, but that is only to be expected. We reach this point, only to pull up the ladder *à la* Wittgenstein.

## A UFO Under Scrutiny

Imagine a species of beings that inhabits this planet whose access to the whole of reality is subtly different to ours. It possesses some of our senses, but it also 'sees' things that we do not and vice-versa. One might imagine that we would find its behaviour difficult to account for.

But not necessarily. Evolutionarily speaking, there might be enough of an overlap between its perception of reality and ours for us to commit an oversight. A surfeit of generosity in interpreting some of its behaviour via H (see above), means we end up interpreting all of its behaviour via H. Part of the problem is the well-known difficulty within behaviourism (sometimes impossibility) of distinguishing behaviour from physics.

It might be objected that this would not happen. We would notice apparently purposeless electrical activity in the creature's brain and this lacuna would alert us to a mystery. This is possible in principle, but I think it is at best far-future neuroscience. And it may not be possible at all. There might always be several candidates ready to hand within our reality-sphere to supply a plausible explanation, and since we can never expect to discover a one-to-one correlation of thoughts and nerve matter, we would never know that we were wrong.

Imagine a gnat on a table whose nervous system is open to scrutiny by a scientist. Every so often, the gnat sees an entity in an area of reality necessarily closed off to the scientist *qua* human. The scientist notes the spike in 'brain' activity, then looks for phenomena in the gnat's visual field; she counts ten things it could have been reacting to. But the spike occurs later when none of those things is present. So she abstracts a property from one of the ten things which one of the new objects in its visual field also exhibits. But then there is another unaccountable spike. Maybe this time she tells herself that the gnat is 'mistaken'. It is clear that we are now deep within the territory of Quine's *Two Dogmas of Empiricism* where "science in its globality is like a force field whose limit points are experiences...a particular experience is never tied to any proposition inside the field except indirectly, for the needs of equilibrium which affect the field in its globality." However adverse the data, our scientist can keep making adjustments to preserve her original position. The latter survives thanks to an indefatigable 'principle of charity'.

But such a principle may be impotent here. The trouble is, behaviour does not occur in discreet packets: it only ever exists as part of an interconnected *network* of behaviour, beginning at birth and ending at death. As investigators, we manage to cut it into discreet packets within which we can apply values only by applying H, but any interpretation based on this must always be at least partly circular. There are always unique features which get discounted and features which remain unseen, and a 'beginning' and an 'end' which are extrinsically circumscribed.

Our 'seeing' of such behaviour may in the end be a Kantian-type thing, and we may ultimately be 'seeing' hardly anything more than H. Not only Quine's two dogmas, but his indeterminacy of translation comes in here, and arguably, any principle of radical translation or interpretation that could conceivably resolve it presupposes the solution to the problem of other minds from analogy. It may be completely useless here.

In the end, it could be that the whole of our understanding of the animal and plant kingdom is a dogma built on the slender basis of a mixture of behaviorism and an assumption that cognitive ability varies directly with brain size. That dogma may be right, but if my analysis here is correct, we can never know for certain. It may be – even *could well be*, given the huge variety of animal species on earth – that some animals are even capable of higher-order thinking, in a way we can never conceive (and can never observe because their agendas are in some way different).

Notice, if this was true, we would not be able to appeal to evolution and natural selection to controvert it – for reasons I have already discussed. Everything would be just as it is. And we would not need to travel to distant planets to discover intelligent aliens. They would already be here among us.

To those who would appeal to Ockham's Razor at this point, I would say: I agree that for practical purposes we have no alternative but to proceed on the assumption that our conventional model of a cognitive hierarchy is correct. But sometimes the razor cuts cleanly, sometimes not. On this occasion, I think it has been ineffectual enough to give us pause for thought. Apart from anything else, it may be that we are hardwired to attribute intelligence based on behaviour. To put it in semi-Kantian terms, 'If you're so smart, how come you ain't rich?' may be part of our *Anschauung*, or 'intuition' of the world. To express it another way, we may be doomed always to anthropomorphise the non-human world, despite our best intentions.

Such an interpretation might find confirmation of a sort in Hume's 1772 *An Enquiry Concerning Human Understanding*. We do not know the sun will rise tomorrow morning, or that the laws of nature will consider forever the same. In the absence of reasons to think otherwise, we suppose they will. This assumption - that phenomena necessarily beyond our purview will endlessly repeat the features of those within - is a psychological, not a logical one. It tells us at least as much about *ourselves* as about the universe.

# TOWARDS SOME KIND OF 'SOLUTION' TO THE PROBLEM OF EVIL

The problem of evil can be posed like this: if God is perfectly loving, God must want to abolish evil; and if God is all-powerful, God must be capable of abolishing evil. But evil exists; therefore, God cannot be perfectly loving and omnipotent. To put it another way, God does not exist. Because by definition, God must be omnibenevolent and omnipotent. If no being possesses those two qualities, that is the same as saying there is no God.

The problem of evil is therefore one of the most powerful arguments for atheism, as opposed to agnosticism. And of course, it has prompted a variety of responses from theists, some more plausible than others, but none especially impressive. We can dismiss Augustine's insistence that evil is a result of humankind's rebellion against God – no one believes the story of the Fall any more – although his accompanying notion, inherited from Plato, that evil is a privation is perhaps more useful. We can also the dismiss appeal to an evil demiurge – a 'devil', 'Satan', or in Gnostic theology, some kind of lesser god – as responsible for evil, because that simply defers the problem. God, as omnipotent, could presumably act to stop such a being.

There are probably only two halfway plausible responses to the Problem of Evil. The first is exemplified in the Biblical Book of Job: God is a mystery to humans; His is a mind so vastly superior to ours that we cannot meaningfully begin to understand its purposes. Even if God told us the solution to the problem of evil, we wouldn't understand it. On this view, faith is God is, to some extent, faith that there is a solution to the problem of evil as posed by humans. The two things – faith in God and faith in the solution to the problem - aren't separate.

The second response is to be found in the writings of Irenaeus, Bishop of Lyon (130-202 CE), particularly *Adversus Haereses*, and Origen (184-253 CE).

According to John Hick, the writer who effectively rediscovered, and arguably reinvented, Irenaeus' theodicy for modern readers, Irenaeus distinguished two stages of the creation of the human race. The first was when human beings were made by God in his *image*. They were not created perfect, but imperfect (or rather 'immature'), at the beginning of a long process of moral and spiritual growth. The second stage of creation is now taking place, and involves human beings perfecting themselves by free interaction with their environment. Eventually, they will attain the *likeness* of God. Human beings are created by God immature instead of perfect because of the positive value of human freedom. A goodness that is the result of freedom is more valuable than a goodness that is ready-made.

For Irenaeus, human beings are created at an epistemic distance from God - a distance in the dimension of knowledge. For human beings to stand in the direct presence of God would mean they could never be free: only where God is hidden and accessible solely through the unconstrained response of faith is human freedom possible. Meanwhile, it would be inconsistent with all this for the world to be a hedonistic paradise. On the contrary, it would have to be governed by regularity, by general laws, which have to be respected, sometimes on pain of death. We need to be able to predict likely outcomes in order to make rational moral choices, and in a world with no fixed laws – where they kept changing so as to avoid causing pain and suffering – our moral growth would be impossible. None of our actions would have moral consequences. We could never harm anyone, even if we tried.

This goes some way towards being a plausible 'solution', and it becomes even more attractive in view of its three corollaries.

1. Sometimes suffering does not educate or improve people, it embitters them. Therefore, any Divine purpose of soul-making that is at work in earthly history must continue beyond this life if it is ever to achieve more than partial and fragmentary success.

2. The goal which God has in store for us must be good enough - beyond our present imaginations - to justify all that has happened *en route* to it.

3. It requires that all human beings shall in the end attain the ultimate blessedness.

Philosophically, I think the last probably hangs on the Socratic claim that no one ever errs willingly. According to Socrates (470-399 BCE), if I make a willing error (ie, if I know what I'm doing is a mistake), then I cannot be said to be 'erring'. I'm doing what I consciously set out to do. Socrates took this to mean that people only did wrong out of ignorance. To truly 'err' is to fail to possess the relevant knowledge. Immoral people truly err. Therefore, they must fail to possess the relevant knowledge. Irenaeus never draws explicitly on this idea, but it would be at least consistent with his thinking to say he holds we err *un*willingly because we are created at an epistemic distance from God. Ultimately, punishing us everlastingly for it might not achieve anything.

This is consistent with what other thinkers have sometimes pointed out. For the Problem of Evil to be genuinely 'solved', it has to be shown that *it does not exist*. A universe in which God merely compensates people for the suffering they have undergone is an imperfect, or faulty, universe. But if the universe is imperfect, its creator must be too. As Friedrich Schleiermacher (1768-1834) pointed out, the idea of a perfect creation going spontaneously wrong is a self-contradiction. It would amount to the self-creation of evil out of nothing.

The dissolution of the problem of evil would require one of two things: either (1) at a deep level, evil and suffering are illusory (certain versions of Hinduism and Buddhism teach this); or (2) evil and suffering do exist, but at a much higher level, they are a component part of a good that would be impossible without them. Option (1) may completely homogenise the universe (eg, so that all *dharmas* are emptiness, as in some Buddhist thinking); the latter would preserve its apparent diversity.

Is (2) the same as saying evil and suffering don't exist? An apparent smudge on a canvas may be resolved on a higher level into a tiny, but essential part of a magnificent painting; yet, taken in itself, the smudge is still what it is.

Yet evil is not like this. If it constitutes an integral contribution to an overall much greater good, how can it be evil?

We sometimes talk, misleadingly, in this connection, of a *necessary* evil, by which we mean some pain undergone in the service of a greater benefit. In order for people to appear in the world, women generally have to undergo the agonies of childbirth.

But the idea of a literally necessary evil – as opposed to necessary suffering - may be incoherent. To deem something *evil* implies that it could have been something other than it was. Hurricanes, earthquakes and man-eating sharks aren't evil, however much suffering they may cause. 'Evil' in this sense, probably *is* a privation, as Augustine thought.

So what *is* evil? If Kant was right – as he probably was - to say there is nothing good in the world but a good will, it would seem the opposite must also be true. Evil, in its essence, surely, is an evil will: the will to inflict gratuitous harm on other sentient beings. And plenty of people seem possessed of an evil will. Hitler, for example, Pol Pot, Jihadi John.

It is difficult for us to get to a dispassionate consideration of this question, because we are acutely aware of the horrendous suffering such people generally cause. But we have already accepted that evil and suffering are not necessarily conjoined. What such people possess - what makes them evil - is an *evil will*. If they had somehow did what they do by accident, or in a dream, we would regard them differently.

How irreducible is the evil will? Could we adopt Socrates' position that such people are actually victims of egregious ignorance?

The normal objection to such an idea is that good and evil have no facts of the matter about them. Socrates notoriously considered moral behaviour to be a skill that could be taught, like carpentry or shoe-making. But, so the objection runs, it isn't. There is no possibility of "ignorance" about it, because there is no knowledge to be had. Morality, if we are pushed to say what it is (and we may reasonably decline), is a mixture of sentiment and prejudice.

As always with anything worth philosophical discussion, there are lots of arguments for both sides. However, in considering the question, How can God permit suffering, we have to posit God as a given. And in that case, there *have to be* moral facts of the matter. In other words, we are considering a question where it makes sense to introduce Socrates' willing error into the mix of possible responses.

And in fact, that may not be so far from what we all do in such cases anyway, even non-religious people. Humanists often tell us that morality is innate in people as evidenced by altruism in apes. That would make great immorality unnatural, and thus arguably, 'erroneous'. People of all faiths and none believe in the universal possibility of contrition, and the actual reform of even the most hardened criminals. Even the most evil will is rarely thought to be utterly incorrigible.

If this is correct, evil may well be a privation, and in that sense a 'nothing'. Could we hold this?

At this point, the emphasis must switch to suffering. One of the biggest criticisms of Irenaeus' theodicy is that it breaks down at a certain point in the reckoning of suffering. Granted, the world has to contain suffering for us to reach moral maturity. But does it have to contain the amount of suffering it actually does? Arguably, there is just *too much* suffering to serve any bigger purpose.

In his *Three Essays on Religion* (1870), John Stuart Mill wrote, "Nearly all the things which men are hanged or imprisoned for doing to one another are nature's everyday performances. Even the love of 'order' which is thought to be a following of the ways of nature is in fact a contradiction of them. All which people are accustomed to deprecate as 'disorder' and its consequences is precisely a counterpart of nature's ways. Anarchy and the reign of Terror are overmatched in injustice, ruin, and death by a hurricane and a pestilence..."

In *River Out of Eden* (1996), Richard Dawkins makes a similar point. "The total amount of suffering per year in the natural world is beyond all decent contemplation. During the minute that it takes me to compose this sentence, thousands of animals are being eaten alive, many others are running for their lives, whimpering with fear, others are slowly being devoured from within by rasping parasites, thousands of all kinds are dying of starvation, thirst, and disease. It must be so. If there ever is a time of plenty, this very fact will automatically lead to an increase in the population until the natural state of starvation and misery is restored. In a universe of electrons and selfish genes, blind physical forces and genetic replication, some people are going to get hurt, other people are going to get lucky, and you won't find any rhyme or reason in it, nor any justice. The universe that we observe has precisely the properties we should expect if there is, at bottom, no design, no purpose, no evil, no good, nothing but pitiless indifference."

Such observations are often presented as a means of fleshing out the problem of evil (probably better termed 'the problem of suffering' now). The claim is that the problem has always been grotesquely understated. A few beings' suffering alone raises that 'problem', but we have far more than a few beings: we have billions and billions of beings in a process that has continued uninterrupted for aeons and which continues with each passing minute. The problem, in other words, is the *sheer quantity* of suffering. Against a small amount, the idea of a benevolent God could conceivably survive – just. But against the *actual* amount, that idea is dead in the water. To suggest otherwise is tantamount to moral blindness.

Let us go back and survey what we have argued so far. Firstly, we have said that evil and suffering are not two sides of the same coin. The only evil thing in the world is an evil will, and an evil will is only efficacious insofar as it creates suffering. In itself, it is arguably a privation. The theological problem of evil, therefore, is really the theological problem of suffering, and it is best captured in a serious consideration of the gargantuan *quantity* of suffering.

Can the problem in this formulation be tackled? I think it can. I think it rests on a confusion between perspectives: suffering as seen from the *outside*, and suffering as seen from the *inside*.

Seeing it from the *outside* means acknowledging that there is a huge quantity of suffering in the world in precisely the way we have just seen. Instrumentally, suffering can be considered an objective phenomenon insofar as it occurs in the countable entities that are embodied individual beings. But to some extent, this is a sleight of hand.

Seeing it from the *inside* means recognising that sufferings cannot be added together, except (relatively weakly) through emotions such as empathy or anticipation. This is suffering in the only sense in which it really exists: as a subjective phenomenon. When I suffer, there is a significant sense in which I suffer alone, and that goes for everyone and everything that has ever suffered. I cannot experience the suffering of the tens of millions of animals that are ripped limb from limb by predators every day, and they cannot experience mine or each other's. Even to the extent that I sympathise with them, or fear for my own life, it is *my* suffering that is under consideration. In a crucial sense, there is only, and has only ever been, one suffering being. To put it another way, although objectively and countably, suffering may be millions of beings wide, metaphysically, it is only ever one individual deep.

Why would we think otherwise? Well, possibly because we are social animals accustomed to thinking in social terms. The *political* problem of suffering really is the problem of quantities of suffering beings added together. We genuinely *can* add sufferings together to consider political, economic and social questions. And in a sense, we must.

But the fact that we can do it in this sense does not mean it makes sense metaphysically. Part of the illusion that it does may stem from the fact that God has often been conceived of as a political being: a king or tribal ruler. We need to slough off this conception if we are to see the problem aright.

Could the problem of suffering have a solution? Possibly. Part of its intractability in the traditional formulation has always lain in the idea that it constitutes a potential infinite. It began to accumulate at a certain point during the emergence of life on earth, and it then looked set to continue indefinitely. If I am right, this is a misconstrual of the metaphysical problem. If there is only ever one suffering being, its suffering is temporally and spatially extremely limited in comparison with the amount of time and space there is. Given that fact, there are a large number of ways the problem might not be so intractable.

# FREE WILL AND LIBET'S EXPERIMENT

Do human beings possess free will? Since Benjamin Libet's experimental work in the 1980s, the answer has often been taken to be a conclusive 'no'. Libet showed that, in a situation in which a subject is required to press a button as a willed action, non-conscious neuronal events always precede the apparently freely willed action, and that – however much the subject might imagine otherwise – in reality, he or she only becomes aware of the 'willed' action afterwards. Human consciousness is not required to explain such actions, only brain activity. Consciousness can be entirely eliminated from the equation, and free will – so the inference goes - is an illusion.

This would support epiphenomenalism, the idea that consciousness has no causative role to play in human action. The mind may *think* it is in charge, but it isn't. It has no more impact on the world than a cloud of chimney-smoke has on the factory below it.

Since Libet, other neuroscientists have reached similar conclusions, backed by experimental research. Itzhak Fried, in the 1990s, showed that desires to move parts of the body could be induced by stimulating parts of the brain with electrodes. Increasing the current actually produced the corresponding bodily movement. So both the desire to do something and the actual doing of it were non-voluntary.

All of this allegedly proves that there is no such thing as free will. We are brain-body unities. Consciousness, and its hallmark concomitant, free-will, are merely non-efficacious by-products of physical events.

Add to this other anomalies, such as sleepwalkers occasionally performing highly exacting tasks unconsciously, and free-will seems to have a major problem.

In this essay, I want to show that the problem of free-will is not a neuroscientific problem at all, or at least, to the extent that it is, it also appears in a different guise, one which neuroscience cannot address. I will also argue that free-will is a reality.

To show that free-will does not exist, it would be necessary to show that, in *every* instance where I imagine I behave freely, I am acting involuntarily. If consciousness is entirely epiphenomenal, it cannot have *any* impact on the world. While neuroscience is a long way from showing this – it may be impossible to do so anyway - it is still true to say that in all experiments where free-will has been put to the test, it has failed to appear.

And isn't that what science is supposed to be? Not a conclusive testing of every scenario, but only a generalizable hypothesis, apparently confirmed by robust experimentation, and not contradicted by any countervailing evidence.

One problem with discussions about free will is a lack of clarity about its meaning of the term. If it simply means we possess the capacity to act randomly, it is probably not worth having. As Paul Henri Thiry d'Holbach (1723-1789) put it, "If in the heat of the dispute a man asks, 'Am I not the master of throwing myself out of the window?' I shall answer him, no; that whilst he preserves his reason there is no probability that the desire of proving his free agency will become sufficiently powerful a motive to make him sacrifice his life to the attempt. If, notwithstanding this, to prove he is a free agent, he should actually precipitate himself from the window, it would not be correct to conclude he acted freely, but rather that it was the violence of his temperament which spurred him on to this folly."

David Hume put it another way. When we talk about free-will, we do not mean something completely undetermined. Rather free-will only makes sense within the confines of a certain determinism. "For what is meant by liberty, when applied to voluntary actions? We cannot surely mean that actions have so little connection with motives, inclinations and circumstances that one does not follow with a certain degree of uniformity from the other, and that one affords no inference by which we can conclude the existence of the other. For these are plain and acknowledged matters of fact. By liberty, then, we can only mean a power of acting or not acting, according to the determinations of the will; that is, if we choose to remain at rest, we may; if we choose to move, we also may. Now this hypothetical liberty is universally allowed to belong to anyone who is not a prisoner and in chains." (*Enquiries Concerning Human Understanding*, Sect. VIII, pt I, 73, p95).

What Hume is defending is a version of Compatibilism. Free-will and determinism are not mutually exclusive. But that is not the same as saying there is no free-will.

Given this sort of an understanding, Fried's experiments may not be so damning for an intelligent understanding of free-will. Who supposes that their desires and instincts are produced freely anyway? When I get an urge to stand up and stretch my legs for a while, I never suppose that I freely produced that urge. When I give in to it, I do so to some extent because I am in its power. My action is not free in the sense of it being what I would have done in circumstances where the urge was not prodding me.

But we need to get outside this kind of discussion, because it does not address the bigger problem. The real problem of free will isn't about whether I am free to move parts of my body; it is about whether I am free to speak up in a meeting, decline a wedding invitation, save my money or spend it, and so on. In other words, where I give myself an order, or make a prescription for myself, and I follow it. And it is, above all, a moral matter. We assume a continuum between the decision to press a button in a laboratory and the decision to betray a friend, but that may be a mistake.

Part of the problem here is that it is not clear what would falsify determinism. What experiment could we possibly devise to prove we are free? What would have to happen, behaviourally, in order for us to know we are free? Presumably, it would always be open to the resolute determinist to claim that we would have exhibited such behaviour anyway.

Imagine two people, A and B. A has an unlimited pile of cards on each of which she writes down an action that B could perform. In principle, there are an infinite number of things she could write down, because the space surrounding B is infinitely divisible. Theoretically, she can keep writing new cards for ever.

Now in practice, B might not want to do some of the things A records, but let's imagine we have a wealthy benefactor C, who persuades B to participate in the experiment for the sake of science. C will bankroll all the more expensive options A suggests, no questions asked. B agrees to participate.

A lays out all her cards in a line of *pairs*. She tells B to choose either card from the first pair, do as it says, then move on to the second pair, do the same there, and continue indefinitely. However, A asks B to choose according to a *system* of B's own devising. (The unseen member of each pair exists solely to prove that there was always something else B could have done.)

B decides to always choose the left-hand card. The first selection tells him to go to Scotland. B does it. The second card tells B to touch his nose to his knee. He does it. And so on.

The cards contain linguistic symbols inscribed on paper: words. B has to read them, translating them into thoughts. His own thoughts.

If B is not free to act – if there is no such thing as free-will - then we have the difficulty of explaining why he is apparently able to do everything A suggests. It is no good objecting that B has *no choice* but to obey A, because that is untrue. He has consented to participate in the experiment, and by reading the cards, he has converted them into his thoughts.

Let us pause here to consider what a determined event or action looks like. Actions are precisely what is under discussion, so we must leave those aside, and simply consider events (because if there is no free will, the distinction between actions and events collapses in favour of the latter). A good example of a predetermined event is when a piece of dry ice, placed on a table at room temperature and pressure, all eventually sublimates. Or another: I add water to sodium and chlorine, and I get salt. Or again: on a mid-autumn day, an apple falls from its tree to the ground.

The characteristic feature of a determined event is that there can be no surprises. Given the combined factors, the outcome is inevitable and foreseeable. The outcome (the final disappearance of the ice, or the appearance of the salt, or the fall from the branch), which occurred at time T, was always predictable much earlier than T.

Now, let us return to A and B. B picks up one of A's cards and touches his nose to his knee, exactly as instructed. Imagine a time T1, half a millisecond before B looks at A's card. Arguably, no analysis of B's brain-state at that point could, even in principle, show that B would touch his nose to his knee. Something must have entered the system from outside, something significant enough to overhaul its entire direction of travel.

In any case, if B is free to obey A, then, all things being equal, A is presumably free to obey B. This presupposes (what is indisputable unless one thinks there is something impossible about B writing 'go to Scotland' and 'touch your nose with your knee' on two different pieces of card) that both A and B are capable of issuing orders. It would then seem very odd to say that A is not capable of obeying *A's own* orders, and B is not capable of obeying B's own. And we have already agreed that the number of possibilities for action that A can choose for B is infinite. So, by extension, it would seem that there is a limitless range of actions for B to choose from in obeying his own orders. In practice, the only ones he won't consider are those excluded by Humean Compatibilism: those that conflict with his ideals, urges or perceived interests.

But in addition to this, B independently decided at the outset only ever to choose the left-hand card. The problem for neuroscience lies in explaining why B may continue to do this many months after his original decision. Habit might be one answer. Neural pathways have been created which are easier to sustain than to disrupt. But that begs the question.

Let us add another element to this thought-experiment. Suppose that, instead of choosing only the cards on the left and sticking with that, B decides to vary his choice. To begin with, yes, he will only choose the cards on the left. But in exactly 23 days' time, he will switch to choosing alternate cards: right, left, right, left. Then in 29 days' time, he will only choose the cards on the right. Then three days after that, he will switch to a fourth system, before finally switching back to the original left-hand row, exactly six months from now.

This is a lot to remember, so he sets his watch-alarm. When it goes off, he remembers what he decided and switches tactics accordingly.

Where are the prioritised neurons here? Well, we could say they were responsible for the original decision to switch, before he set his alarm. But these wouldn't be switching-tactics neurons, because he is not doing that. They would be setting-alarm neurons.

And it is not enough for the alarm itself to later cause him to switch tactics. The decision to switch tactics is mental event, and if such things must be preceded by brain events, we need a prior firing of neurons here too. But how do switching-tactics neurons know to fire in response to B's watch-alarm?

To write the process so it is consistent with Libet, we would have:

1. B's setting-watch-alarm neurons fire (brain event)

2. B sets his watch-alarm (bodily action)

3. B decides to set his watch-alarm (mental event)

4. B's watch-alarm sounds (fact of physics)

5. B's switching-tactics neurons fire (brain event)

6. B switches tactics (bodily action)

7. B decides to switch tactics (mental event)

The problem with this is that when the brain event and the mental event can be reasonably supposed to be almost simultaneous, as in Libet, it makes sense to ask about the order of priority. But it doesn't, so much, when there is a long gap, as for example, if B's watch alarm sounds and he then takes a five or ten minute break before making the first move in his new system. None the less, it may still be that a brain event precedes the relevant bodily action.

But at this point we may reasonably ask the free-will denier exactly what he is denying. As we have seen, B is capable of issuing orders to himself (within the confines of Compatibilism) and obeying them. In theory, he is capable of obeying any number of such orders even when they are set by A and must be, from his point of view, random. Brain events may or may not play a part in the process. The question is: what difference does it make, and in virtue of what lack in B are we entitled to say that he never acts freely?

At this juncture, it may be worth returning to Libet's experiment, because there is something that is generally missed. The researcher tells the subject to press a button and record the time he decided to press. The brain event always precedes consciousness of the volition. But what goes unnoticed is that the subject's button-pushing only makes sense against a prior background in which the decision to push the button has already been made. In obedience to the researcher, the subject has decided (or rather, has been told, and has consented) to press the button before the experiment commences, and his random individual actions in this regard are arguably mere tokens of a more comprehensive mental state: the firm antecedent decision, with which he enters the chamber, to push the button at least once.

If this is true, the true sequence of events isn't

1. brain state   2. button push   3. mental decision/realisation

but rather

4. mental state/disposition   5. brain state   6. mental decision

1 and 3 are obviously totally different kinds of things. But 4 and 6 could be very similar. In any case, the question of when exactly to press the button is an exercise of randomness, and may not bear much relation to free will, if by the latter we understand the making of moral decisions. And the priority of 4 could still allow us to assert a mental exercise of free-will if we so choose.

In fact, Libet's experiment may resemble our thought experiment with A and B more than appears. The researcher plays the part of A, providing an instruction to B to press the button and record the time. Repeat: this happens before the experiment begins. Technically, at this point, B is free *not to press the button at all* – he could resolve, before he even sits down. to disobey A. In that case, there will be no brain activity.

But does anyone imagine this will happen? The fact is that the authority of a scientist in a lab coat partly forestalls the possibility of dissent. In this sense, it may be more useful to compare Libet with sociological experiments such as Stanley Milgram's in 1963 or Leonard Bickman's in 1974, both of which demonstrate that people are more likely to obey a stranger if dressed in a uniform. Here perhaps are the real implications of Libet's work for free will.

In any case, let us go further, because we may be able to show that the conclusion often drawn from Libet's experiment - that free-will is non-existent - is false.

Let us imagine two different experiments:

1. Libet's experiment. A subject is put into a room, wired up to a brain monitor, given a button to press and told to make a record of when he decides to press it.

2. A second experiment. A group of subjects is given the same equipment, but each is asked to decide, individually, in advance of entering the room, *whether he or she will press the button at all*. They are each asked to record that decision on a piece of paper, disclosing it no one, and put that paper into a sealed envelope - again, before entering the room.

We can easily imagine what will happen with Group 2. Each person will enter the room; once inside, he or she will either (i) press the button once or more or (ii) not press the button at all. And it is reasonable to suppose that, providing we have made a selection of truthful and honest people, whether they fall into group (i) or group (ii) will correspond exactly to their written decision as recorded on paper before they entered the room. The written decisions will be separable into two groups which correspond exactly to the two groups of people.

The point is that if two different experiments investigate the same issue, then whatever true conclusion one establishes must be capable of explaining both. So whatever true conclusion we derive from (1), above, must be capable of explaining (2). This is much stronger than merely saying that we have to account for experiment (2). Rather, since we have a true conclusion, it must also be the key to unlocking both experiments.

If the conclusion that emerges from (1) is that human free-will is illusory, then that assertion must be capable of explaining the results of (2). But not only does it look incapable of doing so, it actually seems to favour an equally strong, utterly contrary conclusion. It looks as if we are equally entitled to ask whether (1) can be explained in terms of a conclusion derived from (2) to the effect that we are free.

What might such an explanation look like? The answer is complex because it would seem that presently, we can only talk in terms of the brain: so maybe one part of the brain is capable of making free decisions whose precise execution it delegates to other parts. The first part can decide whether, for example, to walk home or to walk to a pub. Once that decision has been made, the actual walking is passed over to another part, which executes the order to walk on a broadly mechanical basis.

There is a problem in talking about the brain like this, though. The brain is a fairly self-enclosed, self-sufficient chemical-electrical-material system. In principle it can be entirely explained using the laws of physics. Which leaves no room for 'freedom', only causes and effects.

This leads us to the last resort of the free-will denier. She might claim that the entire universe is a deterministic system. Back to our two card players, A and B. The scientific determinist would claim that it was always inevitable to A would create the cards we have described, and that B would choose the cards she chose.

The argument for that position goes roughly as follows: everything in the universe, including humans, is made of a few basic particles. How those particles behave is described by the Mathematical formulation of the Standard Model. It is possible to predict the behaviour of those particles with complete accuracy. In addition to this, we have quantum mechanics, which allows for random jumps. The result is that what we have is a deterministic system with random jumps.

We shall leave aside that 'random' means 'chance' and that a *jump* is an event (suggesting the weird conclusion that the universe is an entirely deterministic system entirely shot through with chance events), and concentrate on the maths.

What is it for mathematics to 'describe' the universe? Or, in fact, can it ever do so? How is it ever possible for scientists to say (as they sometimes do) that their current mathematical model of the world is 'wrong'? And doesn't that possibility hold for all mathematical models of the world?

Arguably, it must do, because the reliability of the model always depends on the *a posteriori* reality. If it didn't, the facts of the universe would be *a priori* truths, like Euclid's theorems. And saying that we could use mathematics to make accurate 'predictions' would be contrived: it would be like saying we can accurately 'predict' that the outcome of 2 + 2 will be 4. The very notion of prediction in mathematical models of the world excludes the perfect rigour required for an incontestable claim that the universe is determined. (Part of that may have to do with the deeper Kantian problem of our inability to ever know the world *as it is in itself,* as opposed to the world *as it appears to us* - since mathematical models can only tell us about the latter.)

One final observation. There is a second, less important problem with Libet's experiment, concerning whether our language of mental states is sufficiently rich to explain what is going on. The subject is required to press a button as a willed action, but sometimes a person may consciously make a decision using all the mechanisms of rational thought, and only later become aware that she has made that decision (a kind of, 'Wait a moment: what on earth have I just *done?*). At the latter point, we are dealing with a kind of second-order consciousness for which there may be no word. True, willing is a conscious matter; awareness of willing may be a different matter. This would require two consciousnesses in the same person at the same time, but, strange though that may sound, it is not wholly counter-intuitive.

As I mentioned earlier, one of the problems with the claim that we do not possess free will is that it is impossible to say, even roughly, what would have to happen to falsify it. A theory without falsification conditions can never be scientific.

But even its verification conditions are obscure. The idea that we have no free-will and all our behaviour is determined doesn't help predict elections, or prevent crimes, or predict wars; it doesn't even tell us what Simon, or Jill, or Billie will do tomorrow, or in ten minutes' time. It's a useless piece of dogma, and arguably harmful.

But that's the beginning of a moral argument.

# Books by James Ward

### General Fiction
*The House of Charles Swinter*
*The Weird Problem of Good*
*The Bright Fish*
*Hannah and Soraya's Fully Magic Generation-Y \*Snowflake\* Road Trip across America*

### The Original Tales of MI7
*Our Woman in Jamaica*
*The Kramski Case*
*The Girl from Kandahar*
*The Vengeance of San Gennaro*

### The John Mordred Tales of MI7 books
*The Eastern Ukraine Question*
*The Social Magus*
*Encounter with ISIS*
*World War O*
*The New Europeans*
*Libya Story*
*Little War in London*
*The Square Mile Murder*
*The Ultimate Londoner*
*Death in a Half Foreign Country*
*The BBC Hunters*
*The Seductive Scent of Empire*
*Humankind 2.0*
*Ruby Parker's Last Orders*

### Poetry
*The Latest Noel*
*Metals of the Future*

### Short Stories
*An Evening at the Beach*
*Wadhurst Ghost Stories*

### Philosophy
*21st Century Philosophy*
*A New Theory of Justice and Other Essays*

www.ingramcontent.com/pod-product-compliance
Lightning Source LLC
Chambersburg PA
CBHW021440080526
44588CB00009B/617